Letters
from the
Home
FRONT
World War II

Barbara Bannister
and Connie Duncan

abbott press®
A DIVISION OF WRITER'S DIGEST

Abbott Press books may be ordered through
booksellers or by contacting:

Abbott Press
1663 Liberty Drive
Bloomington, IN 47403
www.abbottpress.com
Phone: 1-866-697-5310

Because of the dynamic nature of the Internet, any web
addresses or links contained in this book may have changed
since publication and may no longer be valid. The views
expressed in this work are solely those of the author and do
not necessarily reflect the views of the publisher, and the
publisher hereby disclaims any responsibility for them.

Any people depicted in stock imagery provided
by Thinkstock are models, and such images are
being used for illustrative purposes only.

Certain stock imagery © Thinkstock.

ISBN: 978-1-4582-0961-0 (sc)
ISBN: 978-1-4582-0960-3 (hc)
ISBN: 978-1-4582-0959-7 (e)

Library of Congress Control Number: 2013909673

Printed in the United States of America.

Abbott Press rev. date: 06/13/2013

"Hi, Carolyn,"

Carolyn recognized Patty's voice as soon as she picked up the phone.

"Hi, Patty, I'm really looking forward to seeing you next week at Callie's wedding!"

"Me too, but that's not why I'm calling you."

"I hope nothing's wrong. The wedding isn't off, is it?"

"No, you worrywart! It's just that I was up in the attic in the old place in Omaha and guess what I found! In an old cedar chest that I used to call my "hope" chest, I found all of my letters from you back in the 40s. I had saved all of them and had them tied up with a blue ribbon. I started to read the first one and then I thought that if you still had your letters from me it would be fun to read them together."

"I know exactly where those letters are. I was watching a World War II movie the other day and I thought about those letters."

"Bring them with you when you come for the wedding. It'll be fun to remember those days! I'll bet we'll have a million laughs! Don't peek! We'll read them together."

"Boy, that's going to be hard for me! I'm such a snoop."

"I can't wait to see you. In only a week we'll be together. I'm renting a room at the best motel here in town so we can visit (and read!) without bothering the wedding preparations."

"Sounds great! See you then."

Patty hung up and picked up the letters. She stuffed them into her suitcase so she wouldn't forget them.

Patty glanced at the arrivals and departures. "Great! Carolyn's plane is on time!

I wish I could go down to the concourse like we used to. 9-11 really changed things!"

Patty was beginning to think Carolyn had missed the plane as the disembarking passengers hurried by her. But at last she saw her coming, pulling a large black suitcase.

"She must be planning to stay a month," she thought as she ran to Carolyn and hugged her.

"I'm starving!" said Carolyn. "I had to get to the airport in Portland at 4 this morning!"

"Well, it's only ten o'clock here, but we can stop on the way to the motel and have some tea, and you can find something good to eat."

"Anything is better than airline cuisine."

"If you can call it that!"

Later, when the bags were all unpacked they took their iced tea out on to the balcony that overlooked the pool.

"I'm glad you got a motel that had a nice pool. I packed my swimsuit, did you?: Carolyn asked.

"You know what a lousy swimmer I am," said Patty, "But I did pack it. I'll sit on the side and watch you."

"It's a good thing you've got your suit. I'd have made you go in your underwear otherwise."

"You and how many others?"

"Well, let's get started," said Patty. "Your card from Idaho started the whole thing. I was so sad that you were going out west."

"You read first" said Carolyn.

"Here goes!"

July 16, 1941

I'm writing this postcard from Twin Falls, Idaho, as you can see by the picture. We stayed here last night. We should be in Oregon by tomorrow. I didn't get a chance to tell you that we have our new address. It is P.O. Box 45, Mansfield, Oregon. I miss you and Nebraska. Love, Your cousin, Carolyn

Carolyn smiled. "I enjoyed that trip but I was sad too. I didn't want to leave you and my friends. Oregon seemed like the end of the world. I was really happy when your letter got there."

Wabash, Nebraska
July 25, 1941

Dear Carolyn,

I got your postcard from Twin Falls, Idaho. I wish I could have gone with you! I'd love to see all the states you're passing through. The farthest I've been is Omaha to see our Grandma. And once I went to Lincoln to see the Nebraska football team play. Well, I did go on the train to Chicago once with my Nana, but I was only four years old so it was a long time ago.

I miss you so much already. Did you know that Mama and Daddy are getting a divorce? When they told us, it was the saddest day of my life. Callie's too! She and I cried and cried. Daddy said that he and Mama loved both of us but, they couldn't be married any longer even though they were still friends. We are going to live with Daddy and Nana in Wabash. Daddy will teach seventh grade there. Mama is going to work in Omaha. Remember a month ago when we were all together at Aunt Abby's house? I think your mom tried to talk our mom out of leaving. Since they are twins they usually think alike but your mom had no luck this time.

(Patty paused for a moment and Carolyn interjected, "I know. We both hoped and prayed they would get back together, but some good things came of it too. I really envied you the two years you got to spend in Japan that never would have happened without the divorce.

Patty nodded. "Well, I envied you having both parents together and being able to stay in one school through high school."

Patty continued reading,")

I haven't met any kids here yet. We only moved here last week. We have a big yard and a house with an upstairs and a basement. Callie and I have to share a room but we have another room we can use for our toys and books. Daddy has a room and Nana has a room and we have a living room, dining room, kitchen and bathroom. I saw a girl in the house behind us. I hope she's in my grade. Without you here, I will need a girl friend.

Be sure to write and tell us all about Oregon. I never thought you would move so far away! Why did your dad have to go and buy a farm in Oregon? We have lots of farms in Nebraska! Write soon!

Love,

Your cousin, Patty

(Carolyn said, "Most of our farm has been sold for a housing development but we still have a small pasture so we can get down to Orebraska Creek. Do you remember that you helped name that creek?"

"All I remember about Orebraska Creek are those ugly crawdads that we caught there the summer I came to see you," said Patty with a grin. "Now you read the next letter.")

Mansfield, Oregon
August 1, 1941

Dear Patty,

I can't believe Aunt Opal and Uncle Don are getting a divorce. Mama says we just have to pray for them every day. Mama is going to call your mom when we get a telephone.

Our house is on the edge of town. The barns and fields stretch to a creek that has no name. Daddy says that Jessie and I can name it. Jessie wants to call it Little Platte. I think she is homesick too. Since I've never named anything before, I want it to be special so I haven't decided on anything yet.

Daddy likes his job. He is a millwright. He fixes machines that break down in the lumber mill. All of Mansfield smells like fresh Christmas trees because there are dozens of mills around here.

Daddy couldn't wait to show us the ocean so we unpacked the trailer and then drove to the beach. You won't believe your eyes when you see it! The waves crash into the shore. We wanted to go wading but the water was like ice. Daddy said we'd get used to it, but I don't think so! Daddy built a fire of driftwood and we slept on the sand near it. All night long I heard the ocean roar.

When we got home Jessie and I helped Mama unpack the dishes. Jessie did okay for a six year old. She had her 6th birthday at the beach.

Our neighbor, Mr. Yakimoto came over with his daughter, Suki. They brought us a box of peaches from their orchard. So Mama is canning peaches today.

Suki asked Jessie and me to go with her to the swimming pool in Mansfield. We're riding our bikes. It is only a mile. Daddy says he'll teach us how to swim next weekend at the river. We'll have to stay in the shallow end until then.

Miss you. Love, Your cousin Carolyn

(Patty interrupted, "Yes, back then there were hardly any swimming pools. It's hard to learn how to swim in a creek. I didn't take swimming lessons until I was in college and that's too late. I never was any good. Now there are pools in most of the towns and cities. How things change!"

Carolyn nodded, "Yes, Jessie and I both had to take swimming lessons that summer It turned out that Daddy's idea of teaching swimming was to throw us into the river."

Wabash, Nebraska
September 1, 1941

Dear Carolyn,

God hasn't answered my prayers yet because Mama is still in Omaha. I think she is coming to visit at Christmas and maybe she'll stay here then.

I'd love to see the ocean sometime. You are really seeing the world! Well, at least the United States! And Mansfield has a swimming pool! How lucky you are! Remember the little creek we used to get to wade in? That's all there is around here. I'm glad you have a friend! Suki is a pretty name. I never heard that name before.

School starts tomorrow. I can't believe we'll be fifth graders. I've got my hair up in those awful metal curlers so I'll look nice for the first day. I liked it better when Mama put my hair up in rags because they are easier to sleep on. Nana doesn't know how to do it because she says she only had Daddy so she didn't learn how to do girls' hair. I wish I had curly hair. Mama said I did when I was little but when I was five, Nana took me to Chicago on the train. She didn't know how to take care of little girl's hair so she had it cut short. My hair was never curly again. Mama says she'll never forget how I looked when I got off the train. My hair was as straight as can be! Can you remember me with curly hair? I can't.

If I can't have curly hair, I wish I could have looked like Callie. She has blond hair like mine but she has big brown eyes and gets a pretty tan every summer. People always say how cute she is and "What big brown eyes!" I have hazel eyes and I get sunburned if I'm in the sun. And you remember how I get freckles too. Daddy says he likes freckles but I don't.

Callie and I have been to the library here. I've been reading all of the Anne of Green Gables books. I just love them, don't you? I read LITTLE WOMEN, and LITTLE MEN but my favorite book by Louisa May Alcott is JACK AND JILL.

I did meet the girl in the house behind us. Her name is Janie and she is in the fifth grade too. She said she'd walk to school with Callie and me. Her house is really big. It has a big front porch and has a lot of room. I'm glad I have somebody to walk with. We'll take Callie to her room and then she'll show me where the fifth grade room is.

In your next letter tell me what you named the creek behind your house. You could name it the Oregon Platte. Remember the time we roasted marshmallows and hot dogs at the Platte River? They said it was an inch deep and a mile wide. That was fun.

Love, your cousin, Patty

Mansfield, Oregon
September 7, 1941

Dear Patty,

Every year I worry that I will fail my new grade at school. I always do well but I still worry. I also worry about you and your mama and daddy. I hope your next letter will bring good news.

School starts tomorrow. We didn't start as early as you do in Nebraska because the kids pick prunes here and the farmers need them. Next year I'm going to pick too. It will be fun to earn my own money. I'll get to pick strawberries in June, cherries in July, and beans in August. Maybe you can come out next summer and stay with us and earn some money too.

I'm glad you found a friend. Suki and I are becoming good friends too. We rode our bikes to the school last Friday and Mr. Branson, the janitor, let us come in so Suki could show me around. The school is brick and it is tall. It has three stories. The high school is on the third floor. It has a slide that goes from the third floor to the ground. Kids would slide down it if there ever was a fire. While we were there some kids climbed up the slide and rode down on bread wrappers. They came down so fast that they flew off the end. I'd like to try it even if it does look scary. Suki said one boy broke his leg in three places so Mr. Branson yells at them when he catches them on the slide.

(Patty interrupted, "I haven't seen one of those fire escapes in ages. D o you suppose there are still some around?"

Carolyn shook her head. "I know we still have schools with more than one story but I can't remember seeing any of those slides anymore. However they do fire drills now, it can't be as much fun as those old fire escapes were! But I better get on with this letter or we'll never finish reading them all!")

The lower grades are on the middle floor and the toilets, sinks, and showers are in the basement.

There is a big furnace that burns sawdust to heat the building. There is a big room full of sawdust that smells so good that even the bathrooms don't stink.

("I haven't thought of those old sawdust burners in years. We used to see piles of sawdust all over and we even played on the sawdust mountains all the time."

Patty said, "We got to play on hay stacks when we'd go visit a friend on a farm. You don't see haystacks anymore either. Now the hay is harvested all baled up. Baled hay may be neater but it's not as much fun! Well, go ahead and finish the letter.")

Oh, yes, we haven't named the creek yet. We're trying to decide among The Oregon Platte, The Mini-muddy, and the Orebraska. Tell me which you like best.

I better close for now and get ready for tomorrow. I hope I have all my supplies.

With love, Carolyn

Wabash, Nebraska
September 20, 1941

Dear Carolyn,

I got your letter. Picking prunes and the other things sounds like fun and I'd love to earn some money. I hope that I can come out and visit you next summer. How strange that they burn sawdust in the school furnace. You remember that our furnaces burn coal. It doesn't smell good like sawdust but it keeps the furnace hot. Not that we need a hot furnace yet because it is still hot. The nights are getting cooler though and the leaves are starting to turn red. Our sugar maple is beautiful and the big cottonwood's leaves are getting yellow. We raked leaves yesterday and Daddy made a bonfire and burned them last night.

Oh, before I forget, I think I like the OreBraska best as a name for that creek.

School is turning out to be pretty good. I have a pretty teacher named Miss Cook. I like most of the kids in the class. There are about thirty in my class. The girls have different names that I've never heard before such as Coralee, Roseanne, and Jeannice.

Janie is going to be a good friend. I know they must have a lot more money than we have but I don't care. Yesterday after school two boys from our class, George and Richard, followed us home. They teased us by pulling our hair and trying to trip us. We called them pests but they kept it up anyway. When we got to Janie's house, we sat on their porch swing and talked. The boys got tired of that and started showing off by walking on the railing. We thought about doing it but before we got up to try, the boys sat on the railing and tried to see how far they could spit! We said, "Yuck" and told them to go home.

When I got home the house smelled so good! Nana had baked some chocolate chip cookies. They now have chocolate already in chips so you don't have to chop the chocolate up yourself. You can buy a bag at the store. Have you had any yet? They make the BEST cookies. Callie and I probably ate a half a dozen each.

Janie, George, Richard, and Fred came over tonight and we played Andy, Andy, Over. We use our little garage to throw the ball over. Callie played too so we could have even sides. Janie and I got to pick the teams and she chose Richard first. I wanted to pick him but I took Fred and he's a good player too.

Janie and I think we're too old for dolls now, but last Saturday we couldn't think of anything to do so we took all the dolls out in the backyard and played house. Callie has a little washing machine so we washed all the doll clothes. When we saw George and Richard coming down the street, we threw all the doll things in the garage. We didn't want them to see us playing dolls. I think we are too old for that! *(I wish I had those toys now. Children's toys of our era are worth money now days.)*

I hope you like your new school. Tell me all about it in your next letter.

Love, Patty

Mansfield, Oregon
October 2, 1941

Dear Patty,

I don't think we're too old to play with dolls. Jessie, Suki, and I used to pay house almost every day but now we usually play school instead.

Mama says that it is a good idea for you to come out and pick strawberries with me next summer. She said she'd try to work it out with your parents. Won't that be fun? We could pick you up at the train station in Portland.

We haven't had any chocolate chip cookies at our house, but Mama asked the grocer if he would order some for his store. I hope he does. The grocer said they were available since 1939 so it's time they got some. The cookies really sound good.

School is okay so far. Suki and I got to sit together for two days until Mrs. Cummins separated us because she caught us passing notes twice. She's a good teacher though. She reads to us every day. Right now she is reading TOM SAWYER. When Tom had to empty his pocket in the book, she made all the boys empty their pockets onto their desks. It was so funny! Some had twine, fish hooks, pocket knives, and even wads of chewed gum. One boy had a cigar stub and another one had a bunch of marbles that rolled all over the floor. I'm glad I don't have brothers, aren't you?

Mrs. Cummins is teaching us to draw. She says that we draw with our brains not our hands. We find shapes in our classroom and draw them. You'd love her because you're already such a good artist.

Oh, I have to tell you how we start our day at school. It's fun! All the grades, one-twelve, line up in a covered breezeway. Seniors are at the front of the line, then the others in order all the way down to first grade. We say the Pledge of Allegiance and then sing America the Beautiful and the Star Spangled Banner. Sometimes we sing Battle Hymn of the Republic. Then Mrs. Edwards, the principal makes announcements before we all march to our rooms. And we really march. The building almost shakes!

The first thing we do when we get to class is penmanship. I like it because I like to make those circles and up and down strokes. We use dip pens and I hate it when I make a splatter because then I have to start over. The last thing we do is copy a quotation from a famous American. Today we copied something from Thomas Paine's "Common Sense."

One of the girls in my class is called Patsy. I told her that you are called Patty. She said her real name is Patricia just like you but her mother hates the name Patty so she won't let her be called that. Patricia lives seven miles from town. She wants Suki and me to ride our bikes out to her house on Saturday. I asked Mama and she didn't say no. I'll wait and see what Daddy says when he gets home.

Daddy is making a sign to put by the creek. It will say The OreBraska Creek.

Daddy bought a piano and Mama is going to find a teacher to give me lessons.

I miss those sugar maples. Send me a leaf in your next letter. I'm sending you a leaf of vine maple that grows by the creek.

Love, your cousin, Carolyn

Wabash, Nebraska
October 15, 1941

Dear Carolyn,

Thank you for the leaf. I could tell it was once a pretty red but it kind of dried up.

I've really been busy. I've started taking piano lessons, joined the Campfire girls, and Nana made us join the L. T. L. which is short for Loyal Temperance Legion. At the meetings we have to

17

promise to never smoke or drink alcohol. We sing songs with silly verses like, "I bought some beer for fifty cents, goodbye my money goodbye. It made my auto jump the fence, goodbye my auto goodbye. Bye money bye-o, Bye good sense bye-o, Bye auto bye-o, because of beer and a fence." I think it's kind of a stupid song and I don't really even need to go to L.T.L. since I don't intend to smoke or drink. The only one I know who drinks is our Uncle Pete. He took Callie and me to a tavern once and he bought himself a beer and Callie and me an orange crush. Nana was so mad at him for taking us to a TAVERN that he never did that again!

Daddy smokes but since he is a teacher he isn't supposed to so he has to walk home to smoke in his room. It isn't really very far here but you remember when we lived out in the country when I was in the first grade? Then he had to walk a mile back home and blow the smoke out the window. If he got caught smoking he could be fired. That's too much trouble. No smoking for me!

(Carolyn laughed. "Times change. When I first started teaching the staff could smoke in the staff room, then when the rest of the staff complained, smokers had to smoke in the furnace room. Then after the surgeon general said how bad smoking was for your health, smoking was banned from school

property. We're right back now how it was when your dad had to walk a mile home to smoke!"

Patty added, "Back then teachers could not drink alcohol even in a restaurant and you couldn't be seen in a tavern! But I'll go on with the letter.")

What a coincidence that you're going to take piano lessons too. I love taking piano lessons. The teacher just lives down the street. The only trouble is having to go inside to practice just when Callie, Janie, George, Richard and I are having so much playing Andy, Andy, Over or Kick the Can. Every night at eight o'clock Nana calls me in to practice my piano lesson. It feels so good outside because the air is getting cold and the leaves are all crunchy on the ground. It feels hot and stuffy in the house and besides that I can hear the other kids outside having fun. Even Callie doesn't have to come in and she's younger than I am. She gets to take piano lessons next year and then she'll have to come in before I do. Ha ha!

Janie, Callie, and I are planning a Halloween party. We sat outside last Saturday and planned it. We're going to have it in our basement and we're going to decorate with crepe paper. We'll try to make it spooky. We are writing invitations and telling everyone to wear a costume. Callie is going as a gypsy and I've got a skeleton costume. I know I'd look better as a gypsy or princess or something but I don't care. A skeleton costume will be more fun. I've never had a Halloween party before. In the town where we used to live the big boys dumped over out houses or soaped windows but we just went trick or treating to a couple of places. I think a party will be fun. Are you planning anything for Halloween?

("You know, Patty," Carolyn interrupted. "I think we were lucky to have our childhood before all the technology of television, computers, and cell phones because we had to be responsible for our fun."

"That's right," Patty agreed. "We used to have so many parties and get-togethers and that just doesn't happen anymore.")

I'm putting one of the red leaves from the sugar maple in the envelope for you. I pressed it between waxed paper so it will stay nice.

Love, your cousin, Patty

Mansfield, Oregon
October 25, 1941

Dear Patty,

Thank you for the sugar maple leaf. I pinned it to my wall.

We really are a lot alike because I love the piano too. Mama found us a piano teacher. Jessie has to sit and listen and then I have to teach her since Mrs. Jones, the piano teacher won't teach her because she says Jessie's hands are too small.

Your nana would hate Mansfield, There are three taverns. One, The Log Palace, is so evil that even Mama will cross the street so she doesn't have to walk in front of it. A lot of loggers and mill workers spend much of their time in the taverns.

Mama and Daddy are making root beer for Halloween. They are inviting some friends and their families for dinner and a party. Mama doesn't want us to trick or treat this year until she knows more about our neighbors. For the party Mama is going to bake meat loaves inside small pumpkins carved into jack o'lanterns. Isn't that clever? Your party sounds like fun. Are you inviting only girls or are boys coming too? I think Richard is kind of your boyfriend. Am I right?

I'll get to taste chocolate chips soon because Mr. Benson, our grocer, got some chocolate chips.

He had to buy twenty-four so Mama agreed to buy twelve of the packages. She is making cookies for Jessie's and my school Halloween parties.

Suki told me today that her family is going to sell their farm and move back to Hawaii. I am so sad. Patricia and I are friends at school but not like Suki and me, because Patricia is never allowed to come to my house. I don't know why her mother won't let her go play anywhere! I rode my bike to her house once but since then the Oregon rains have come and Mama says I can't go now. Daddy drove me there once and he talked to her dad but she still isn't allowed to visit with any of her school friends in their homes. Doesn't that sound kind of strange? Poor Patricia!

("Patricia's mother likely would have home-schooled Patricia in this day and age, but it wasn't an option then. Do you know whatever happened to her"

"The last I heard she was a reporter for a California newspaper. I think she went to California to get away from her mother!")

I'm going to go read my book now. I'm reading REBECCA OF SUNNYBROOK FARMS. It's a great story. Have you read it? I know you'd like it.

Love from your cousin, Carolyn

Wabash, Nebraska
November 2, 1941

Dear Carolyn

The Halloween party is over and it was so much fun! It was lucky that Halloween was on a Friday this year so we didn't have to go home early because of school the next day. We had both boys and girls at the party. There were six boys and eight girls. Nana made pumpkin shaped cookies and punch. We had the washtub filled with water and there were apples floating in it. We each had to try to get an apple. The boys were all getting one but none of the girls were. I watched and saw that the boys put their heads under water and pushed the apple against the side of the tub so they could get their teeth in it. I tried it and it worked! I got the apple but I also had wet hair hanging down my back for most of the party. When we turned out the lights we passed around a bowl of "eyeballs" which were really peeled grapes, and then some cold spaghetti which we said were intestines. The girls squealed but the boys pretended they weren't scared. Then while the lights were still off we told ghost stories. I told the one about being on one step, and getting closer and closer until you say, "I got you!" Some of the others made up good ones. After we ate it was almost eleven o'clock so everyone went home. Richard gave me a kiss on the cheek in the dark. Or at least I think it was Richard. I slapped whoever did it! Did you have fun on Halloween?

I liked "REBECCA OF SUNNYBROOK FARMS too. I'm reading EMILY CLIMBS right now which is another one by Montgomery. You know, the one who wrote ANNE OF GREEN GABLES.

Mama says she wants us to come to Omaha and have Thanksgiving with her and our Grandma and Aunt Ruby. I wish you could come too. Grandma is your grandma too and Mama and Aunt Ruby are your aunts so we'll all miss you. Callie and I will go there and back on the train. We've never been on a train with just the two of us. Callie has never been on one at all. We are excited about it.

In school we have been going down to a room in the basement and doing woodworking things. We are making a bread board for our mothers for a Christmas present. The boards are all cut out now and we're starting to sand them. When they're smooth we're going to paint decorations on them. I hope mine turns out all right.

I'm sorry Suki is moving away. I know you will miss her. You'll have to find a new best friend.

Write soon and tell me all about your Halloween.

Love, your cousin, Patty

Mansfield, Oregon
November 13, 1941

Dear Patty,

Those Oregon rains that I heard about are here! Everything feels damp. The wood stove in our parlor is fired up day and night. I have to help Daddy fill the wood bin on the porch so Mama doesn't have to lug it up the back steps. The wood shed is attached to the house and the garage is attached to the wood shed.

Your Halloween party sounds great. Did your dad and Nana stay upstairs and let you have the party in the basement with just kids down there? The bobbing for apples sounds like fun. I guess you missed when you tried to slap Richard for that kiss. I think maybe he is your boyfriend.

Halloween is a big event here too. All the merchants wear costumes except for our grocer, Mr. Benson. When we asked him why he didn't have a costume he said that his costume was perfect for a grocer. When we were there Mama bought the chocolate chips and then took them home and made cookies. She took them to both my class and Jessie's class for our Halloween party. Everyone loved them.

The Halloween dinner was fun too. Mama invited the McIntosh family and the Robbins family. Both those families live around here. Johnny and

Jackson McIntosh are a year ahead of me in school. They are twins but they don't look alike. They are usually loud and rowdy but at our house their hair was slicked back and they sat quietly and actually behaved. Mama thought that they were "perfect little gentlemen!: A lot she knows! We played Monopoly and checkers. The grownups rolled up the rugs and danced. Jackson asked me if I wanted to dance. I told him I didn't know how. Im glad he didn't offer to teach me. Now Jesse keeps teasing me, "Carolyn has a boyfriend, Carolyn has a boyfriend!" If I ever do have a boyfriend it won't be Jackson!

On Armistice Day we had an all-school assembly. The high school drama class presented a play and then we sang together. We sang COLUMBIA THE GEM OF THE OCEAN and YANKEE DOODLE DANDY and other patriotic songs. I liked it because I always like time out of school work to sing. Afterwards Mama met Jesse and me and took us to the Kozy Korner Cafe. We had grilled cheese sandwiches and tomato soup. It was funny because that is what Mama fixes at least twice a week. I guess it tastes different to Mama if she doesn't have to make it.

I wish I could go to Omaha to be with you and my aunts and Grandma for Thanksgiving but of course I can't. I know it will be exciting for you to go on the train.

We have a hundred gallon fish tank in our room at school. It has a balance of plants and animals. We are supposed to watch and see nature's balance. I think the goldfish eat the guppies. I hate that! It must be scary to be a guppy.

Daddy just came in and said I have to turn out the light and go to bed. It's a school day tomorrow.

Love, your cousin, Carolyn

Wabash, Nebraska
November 22, 1941

Dear Carolyn,

Guess where I am! You'll never guess I bet! I'm on a train with Callie going to Omaha to spend Thanksgiving with Mama and our grandparents. Callie is sleeping next to me. She's missing all the fun. I'll wake her up when I finish this letter. She's probably sleepy because we just ate the big lunch Nana fixed for us . . . fried chicken, bread and butter, cookies and an apple.

Have you ever ridden on a train? It's fun to be weaving back and forth when I go back to get a drink out of the little paper cups. It's kind of hard to walk even if it is fun. I went back and tried to bring a cup of water and spilled it all over my new shoes.

The porters are so nice to us. They keep coming by to see if we're okay. The conductor just came by and said that the next stop was Omaha so I better quit writing and wake Callie up. We'll need to get our coats on and have the porter get our suitcases down from the rack. I'll finish this at Mama's.

November 24, 1941

We're at Mama's apartment now. It is a cute little place and near the Wonder Bread bakery so outside it smells like fresh-baked bread. Mama took us to a movie at the Paramount last night . . . It was "Dumbo" and I liked it but Callie loved it. I just love the Paramount theater because the lights in the front look like they're chasing each other. They are so pretty. The inside of the theater looks like a castle.

Mama might take us to Brandeis tomorrow and get us a new dress to wear in the Christmas program at school. I can't wait to get to Grandma's and see everybody.

I'll tell you all about it in my next letter.

Happy Thanksgiving,

Love, your cousin Patty

Mansfield, Oregon
November 29, 1941

Dear Patty,

I wish I could have been with you at Grandma's. "Dumbo" hasn't come to Mansfield yet. The theater shows two different movies each week. I get to go most of the time so I'll see Dumbo when it comes.

We went to Aunt Maude and Uncle Karl's for Thanksgiving. Aunt Maude is a wonderful cook. She picks out the best turkey and feeds it special grains for three weeks before Thanksgiving so it's extra tender.

The McIntoshs were invited too, probably because they are from Lincoln, Nebraska. We seem to find a lot of people from Nebraska to be our friends.

Before dinner we kids played in the huge barn. We climbed a ladder up to the loft and sat on a long rope which was knotted to a big iron hook. We swung across the barn and then pushed against the other side of the barn to get us back to the loft. It was scary but fun. We pretended to be circus trapeze artists. Once Jessie forgot to push off on the other side so she didn't get back to the loft. She was hanging in the middle of the barn and it was a long way down. Jackson found a smaller rope hanging nearby and he swung across the barn and on the way back he grabbed her rope and she got back to the loft. He didn't jump off though so now he was hanging in the middle of the barn. He yelled and screamed that he was going to fall and he did. Then I started to scream. I climbed down the ladder and ran to see if he was all right. He was lying so still that I thought he was dead! When I reached him he sat up and yelled, "Boo! I'm dead!"

I was so mad that I told him that I hoped he would choke on the turkey. Then I worried all through dinner that he would and it would be all my fault. The worst part was that Jessie had to go and tell everybody about how Jackson had saved her life. And now Mama thinks Jackson is more wonderful than ever. To make it even worse, Aunt Maude and Uncle Karl thought the joke Jackson played on me was funny.

When I told Suki about it, she told me that she thinks Jackson is cute and that he has a crush on me. I think I hate him!

My grandma and grandpa Schmidt are visiting family in Germany. Daddy and Uncle Karl are worried about them because the Nazis are in control of Germany and Daddy says they are dangerous. I hope Grandma and Grandpa get home safely. They plan to visit us at Christmas.

The Montgomery Ward and Sears Roebuck Christmas catalogs came last week. Jessie and I are going through them and marking everything we would like to have.

Mama told Jessie that Santa's sleigh isn't big enough for all she chose. What I really want is bronze dog head bookends. Have you made a Christmas list yet?

Write soon!

Love, Carolyn

("Why in the world did you want bookends? What an innocent time that was. We had no idea what was to come!"

Carolyn shrugged, "Who knows why I wanted bookends but I did!")

Wabash, Nebraska
December 7, 1941

Dear Carolyn,

What a terrible day. It started like any Sunday. Nana took Callie and me to Sunday School and then we stayed for church with her. When we got home, Daddy was in his room listening to the radio. He came downstairs and told us all to come sit in the living room. Then he told us that the Japanese had bombed Pearl Harbor and we would probably soon be at war. I had never heard of

Pearl Harbor so I asked him where that was. He said it was in Hawaii. I know what war is and I'm frightened. He said there will be changes for all of us. He said he was going to go down and enlist in the navy. When he said that Callie and I started to cry but he said for us not to worry. Later Nana said that maybe the navy wouldn't take him because he had children.

Before all this happened I was going to tell you about the trip to Omaha. It was so much fun and I was so glad to see Grandma and Aunt Ruby and Uncle Bill. Our cousin, David, was there too. He is a senior in high school so I thought he wouldn't pay any attention to Callie and me, but he did. He took us for a ride in Uncle Bill's car and we got to see the holiday decorations in downtown Omaha. Of course there was a lot of snow and he also helped us build the biggest snowman on the street. Mama took our picture beside it and I'll send it to you so you can see the snowman and also how big David is now. Our dinner was good too but we didn't have any exciting times in the barn like you did. I think Suki is right. I think Jackson does like you or he wouldn't bother to play a joke on you. And I think you like him, don't you?

(Patty stopped reading and said, "You used to like him a lot, didn't you? Whatever happened to him?

Carolyn shook her head sadly. "I did like him a lot. I was devastated when I heard he was killed in the Korean War even though we went our separate ways after high school. I see his twin brother Johnny when I go back to Mansfield to visit Jessie."

Patty said, "How sad for Johnny and the family. They were so close."

She picked up the letter and began reading again.)

We got our Christmas catalogs too. I circled a red sweater and a new jacket. I also would like the Pit game. Everybody says it is so much fun. We played Pick Up Sticks at Janie's house and that was fun so I circled that. Callie circled a big baby doll that has eyes that can not only open and shut, but can also roll side to side.

I wonder what it will be like at school tomorrow. Everybody will be so excited and worried. Maybe the teacher will talk about it with us.

It must be even more frightening for you on the coast because you are so much closer to Hawaii. Write and tell me all about what is happening there.

Love, Patty

Mansfield, Oregon
December 12, 1941

Dear Patty,

Already I hate the war. How our lives have changed! Last Sunday we were eating breakfast when the program was interrupted to announce the attack on Pearl Harbor. That afternoon Mr. Yakimota came over to talk to Daddy. He had heard that Americans citizens of Japanese descent will be put in special jails. They can't move to Hawaii because of the war so they will move to Vancouver, Canada with Mrs. Yakimoto's sister. That way they won't be put in the jails.

Later I asked Daddy why they would be put in jails and he said that the government was afraid that some of them might be spies for Japan. Anyway when he came, he signed his farm and livestock to Daddy until the war ends and they can return. So now we have thousands of chickens to take care of as well as twelve more cows. Mama spends all her time gathering eggs and then candling them, you know, holding them up to a light to be sure they are clear. Then she washes them and packs them into egg trays. Jessie and I gather eggs too when we get home from school. I hate chickens! They peck your hand when you reach into their nest. Mama won't let us complain though. She says we have so much and that

34

we make money from those eggs. Mama puts part of the money into a special account for the Yakimoto family. Daddy gets up two hours earlier every day to milk all the cows before he goes to work. We only sell the cream so Mama also has to separate the cream from the milk and then sterilize everything. It is so much work. Jessie and I help as much as we can.

It is so dreary here in Oregon with all the rain. And now we can't even see the neighbor's houses at night because every house has to have blackout curtains to prevent being seen in case of a Japanese attack. I haven't seen any blue sky for weeks and I'm really lonesome for Nebraska and some sunshine.

Is Richard still your boyfriend? Jackson's brother, Johnny, told Jessie that Jackson bought a Christmas present for me. What should I do? I'm afraid to buy one for him because maybe his present is just a joke. Let me know what you think. Write soon because Christmas is near and I really don't know what to do.

Love, your rain-soaked cousin Carolyn

Wabash, Nebraska
December 19, 1941

Dear Carolyn,

I'm sorry that Suki has to move. I hope they'll be able to move back some day. Is she scared to be moving to Canada? We don't have any Japanese people around here so I haven't had any friends that had to leave. And as to a present for Jackson, I don't think you have to get him anything. If he wants to give you a present, just say, "Thank you."

Already things are changing. There are signs up in the store windows and at the post office. There is one of Uncle Sam pointing his finger right at you. It says "Uncle Sam wants You!" I know it means young men that can join the army, navy, or marines, but it makes me feel like I should be doing things too. Yesterday we had good news because we found out that Daddy was not allowed to enlist in the navy. He has one eye that is blind so they would not take him. You can't tell that it is blind but he has had it since he was a baby. I'm glad that he doesn't have to go. We also had good news that Mama is going to come and visit over Christmas. Callie and I are planning ways to talk her into coming back to stay.

We went Christmas shopping last week. Callie and I bought Mama a bottle of Blue Waltz perfume and Daddy a bag of licorice. That is the only kind of candy that he likes. I finished that breadboard in school for Nana. It is pretty but it took the class a month to make them. First we had to sand it until it was smooth, then the next week we painted flowers around the outside, and the last thing we did was shellac it so it would stay nice. We did that a week ago because we wanted it to be really dry before we wrapped it. Today was the last day of school before Christmas vacation so we wrapped them up in paper that we had made by painting Christmas trees on butcher paper. The last hour of the day we had a party. We drew names a couple of weeks ago so we exchanged presents at the party. We were not allowed to spend more than twenty-five cents for the gift. We played musical chairs and then we had decorated sugar cookies that Nana sent and Richard's mom brought chocolate milk. (And no he's not my boyfriend!)

(Carolyn laughed. "You were right! He's not your boyfriend, he's your husband!" Patty laughed too. "We went through a lot before that happened!" She returned to the letter.)

When it was time to go home we saw that it had started to snow again. The boys followed us home and threw snowballs at us along the way. We didn't want to stop and throw some at them because our hands were full with our present we'd gotten at the party and also with the wrapped breadboards. We'll have a snowball fight with them some other time. Luckily the snow was soft and so the snowballs didn't hurt. I'm glad we'll have a white Christmas. I can't remember a Christmas when there wasn't any snow.

When we got home and went in the house it smelled like Christmas. The balsa tree we got last Saturday smelled so good. Daddy, Callie, and I decorated it Saturday night. We found the box of ornaments and put them on after Daddy was finished putting on the lights. I wanted to have all blue lights because I saw a tree in a window that had that and it looked so pretty but Daddy said we had to use the lights that we had so we have all colors. I really don't like putting on the icicles. It takes so long and Daddy wants us to put them on one at a time. When he wasn't looking Callie and I threw several on at once. After the tree was decorated Nana brought out a big bowl of popcorn and we ate it while we listened to the radio.

Sunday night is our Christmas program. The fifth and sixth grades have all the speaking parts. Doris got to be Mary even if she has blond hair and I think Mary had dark hair. She is the tallest in the Sunday School so maybe that is why. Jane and I are angels so we have to say a few lines and then we have to sing a duet. We're singing "Silent Night." I'm singing alto. It's the first time I've ever done it in a program. Callie's class is singing "Away in a Manger". Mama is coming on the train on Saturday so she'll get to be at the program. I can't wait!

Tell me all about your Christmas in your next letter.

I am sticking in a Christmas card I made for you. I wish I could send you a present but Callie and I used up all the money we could save from our allowance on the presents for Daddy and Mama.

Merry Christmas and love from your cousin,

Patty

("Hasn't Christmas decorating changed. I don't think they even sell icicles anymore?" Patty nodded. "If you asked for icicles now you'd get those hanging lights for the outside of the house. And inside there are fiber optic singing carolers and artificial trees and the tiny lights instead of the big lights we had. I did get to decorate with only blue lights one year but now I want all the old decorations that we had through the years.")

Mansfield, Oregon
December 23, 1941

Dear Patty,

I got your letter a few minutes ago and I'll write right back so it can be mailed before Christmas.

Thank you for your advice on my "problem". I don't have to give Jackson a gift because Mama made a box of Christmas cookies and candy for the McIntosh family. Anyway, so far Jackson hasn't given me a gift either. I still think it was just a joke.

Our school Christmas program was on Friday, the nineteenth. It was also the last day of school before Christmas vacation. The program was an all-school musical with each class singing a special song. Jessie's class sang "Santa Claus is Coming to Town," and my class sang "Oh Little Town of Bethlehem" and "What Child is This?". The program ended with the school and the audience all singing Christmas carols. After the program the parents served coffee, tea, punch, and Christmas cookies. It was so wonderful. Mama, Jessie, and I sang carols all the way home.

(Patty interrupted, "That wouldn't happen now. Now the public schools can only have winter programs. Christmas carols and the Christmas story are not allowed.")

Last weekend Jessie, Daddy, and I went down to the creek and walked along the bank until we found a perfect Douglas fir, just a little taller than Daddy. We cut it down and took it home. It was the first time we ever cut our own Christmas tree. It would have been perfect if we could have had Nebraska snow instead of Oregon rain. We were a muddy mess by the time we got home and Mama made Daddy hose off the tree and our galoshes before we could come in the house. We had to let the tree dry off before we could decorate it. We decorated it that night and listened to Christmas music.

The tree smells so good and is so pretty that we can almost forget how hectic our lives have become.

We heard last night on the radio that Japanese submarines were sighted off the coast of Astoria. There is talk that the Japanese will invade the west coast. Daddy says it is unlikely because they seem to prefer islands, like the Philippines and Hawaiian islands.

I'm glad Suki is in Vancouver because people are saying such awful things about the Japanese. Suki's family isn't like that at all. I got a letter from her yesterday telling about her school and her neighborhood. She hasn't made any friends except among her cousins and other Japanese families. They have formed their own school with a Japanese teacher because they are afraid there is anger against all Japanese even in Canada.

(Patty interjected, "Do you ever hear from Suki?"
"I have visited her and her family in Vancouver a few times over the years. She is married to a banker and has two daughters. She has a slight Canadian accent." Patty said, "What does she think about

41

the Japanese internment camps during the war?"
"It isn't something that we've ever talked about
but I think it was a disgrace and an injustice. I
remember being worried that we would be put into
camp because we were Germans." Patty nodded.
"Yes, it was because the Japanese were easy to
identify but the Germans looked like the rest of us
so they weren't interned. I'm glad it never happened
to you!")

The only thing funny about Pearl Harbor is that
Jessie thought that Pearl Harbor was a woman
because Mama's name is Pearl. Jessie told Jackson's
brother, Johnny, that the Japanese had bombed a
poor woman named Pearl Harbor. Daddy explained
to her what a harbor is. Since there are no harbors
in Nebraska and we haven't been to one here, of
course she didn't know what one was!

Mama baked ginger bread cookies. I think they
are cool enough now so we can decorate them as
Christmas trees, Santas, and gingerbread boys and
girls. We'll get to eat the broken ones. I better go
before Jessie eats them all!

Merry Christmas from your cousin in Oregon,
Carolyn

Wabash, Nebraska
January 3, 1942

Dear Carolyn,

I wrote 1941 first and had to erase it. I hope it will be a good year and that Mama will come home and the war will be over.

I don't think Mama is coming home though. We did have a great Christmas together. Mama got here in time for our Christmas program at church. It seemed like everybody in town came. Everyone did a good job and nobody forgot their lines, which was a surprise. After the program Santa came in and stood by the Christmas tree. All of us kids came up and he gave us a sack filled with Christmas candy, peanuts, and an orange. Afterwards, Nana, Mama, Daddy, Callie, and I walked home through the snow. The Christmas trees in the windows looked so pretty. It was cold but it felt good after being so hot in that angel costume. On Christmas morning Callie and I were the first ones up but we had to go back to bed while Daddy got the furnace in the basement going. When we finally got to get up it was still dark so everything looked so Christmasy with just the tree lights. I got a pretty red sweater and a Pit game. Callie got the big doll she wanted and a Pick-up-Sticks game. Mama gave each of us a pretty gold bracelet that had a heart that opened up and we could put

43

a picture in it. After breakfast Daddy and Mama played our new games with us. We had so much fun. Later that night we all went to Daddy's room and talked. Mama said she and Daddy had decided that she should still stay in Omaha. Since she didn't mention that word—divorce—Callie and I are still hoping that we'll all be together again soon. Nana is good to us and we love her but we miss Mama too. She left the next morning on the train. She said we would come to see her at Easter. Afterwards we sat in the dark by the lighted Christmas tree and watched the snow come down outside. Then we turned on the lights and sang Christmas carols that I played on the piano. Nobody seemed to care it I hit a wrong key once in awhile. It was a very nice Christmas. I was happy and even forgot that there is a war and Mama and Daddy aren't together anymore.

On New Year's Eve we begged Daddy to let us stay up until Midnight so we could see the new year start. He said we could read in bed until the new year. Well, we didn't make it. Callie fell asleep and I was sure I could stay awake until midnight but I didn't. I wonder how old I'll be before I get to say "Happy New Year" at midnight!

(Carolyn laughed. "We thought then that staying up until midnight on New Year's eve was so grownup, didn't we? But how long has it been now since you've

stayed up past midnight on New Year's eve?" "Maybe it's been ten years.")

Callie and I made our resolutions. Daddy said we should. We decided that we would not have any fights and I decided that I would try to not complain when I had to practice my piano lessons. Callie decided she would try to make her allowance last all week.

Daddy said that rationing is going to start this month. That means we can only get a few gallons of gas each month. He said that tires are rationed too and that probably other things will be rationed next. I guess it is because the army and navy and marines need the gas and the rubber. The war seems far away but it is going to be different here too. Janie's big brother is going in the army next week. She told me about it yesterday and she cried when she told me.

I hope you had a great Christmas. Did you get your bookends you wanted? And did you get to stay up until midnight on New Year's Eve?

Love from your cousin, Patty

Mansfield, Oregon
January 10, 1942

Dear Patty,

It was strange to wake up on Christmas morning and not have any snow. At least it didn't rain so I got to ride my bike.

We had custard, home-canned peaches, and sweet rolls for Christmas breakfast. Mama already had a big turkey in the oven. I wish you could have seen our tree! It was the most beautiful one we've ever had. It was so tall it reached the ceiling. Mama beat up ivory flakes until they were thick and foamy and we frosted the branches with it. Then we sprinkled the foam with silver glitter. It looks just like the branches are covered with snow. We have to be careful not to bump the tree because this fake snow is just like real snow—it falls off onto the floor. Daddy makes Mama save all that falls because he says soap will be hard to get if the war continues for very long. He says that soap and the stuff they make bombs with all use fat and oil. Our grandmother's "Cleanliness is next to Godliness" is not going to work if we don't have any soap!

Aunt Maud, Uncle Karl and the entire McIntosh family came to Christmas dinner. Dinner was delicious but supper leftovers were even better because we had all the Christmas breads, cookies, pies, and cakes. My favorite is springerli cookies because I love licorice just like your dad.

When the McIntosh family was leaving, Jackson gave me the present. I was so embarrassed that I stuck it into my pocket and he ran for their car. I went to my room to open it because I still thought it could be a joke. It wasn't a joke! It was a beautiful little locket with his picture in it. I didn't tell Mama. I'm not sure I should keep it. What do you think? I know I'll never be able to wear it if I don't tell Mama about it and in the meantime where can I keep it where snoopy Jesse won't find it?

Yes, I got my bookends and I love them! But I didn't stay up until midnight on New Year's Eve. The whole family went to bed at ten o'clock. We are so busy taking care of our place and also the Yakimoto place that we are too tired to stay up very late at night.

I'm so mad I could spit! The girls at school said that Sukie's family were spies and that they had been arrested. Some said that they had escaped on a Japanese submarine. I said, "That's ridiculous! Sukie doesn't speak Japanese and her family only speaks English at home."

Now some of the girls call me a Jap lover because I defended her. They even call me a traitor. One girl, Margaret, defended me. Later she asked me to jump rope with her at recess. Now that Suki is

47

in Canada I'm glad to have someone to be friends with me.

I didn't know about the gas rationing because we haven't been using the car very much. I ride my bicycle to school and Daddy and Mama are too busy to go anywhere.

Write soon.

Love, Carolyn

(Patty put down her stack of letters and shook her head. "Jap lover! Can you imagine saying something like that today? Maybe some things have improved."

Carolyn nodded, "And poor Jessie was called a four-eyed Kraut when she had to get glasses just because our name is Schmidt."

"And now Japan and Germany are among our strongest allies. Our occupations were humane and built up the countries." Patty picked up her letters. "Let's go on reading or we'll never get finished.")

Wabash, Nebraska
January 19, 1942

Dear Carolyn,

I know you're not a traitor! What a terrible thing for those girls to say! Didn't they know Suki too, just as you did? Did you tell them that she went to Canada because they were afraid that people here would be mean to them just because they are Japanese? But it was nice that Margaret defended you. You need a good friend now that Suki is gone.

AND it was exciting that you got a present from Jackson. I didn't get a present from Richard, but he did give me a kiss on the cheek under the mistletoe in the church basement the night of the program. I ran off right away to put on my angel costume and I think he went to get his costume on too. Or maybe he just stayed there and kissed all the girls!

We went ice skating last weekend at the old brickyard pond. I can skate pretty well if I'm going forward but I can't skate backward yet. Richard tried to show me and so did Janie but I just can't. The boys like to play crack the whip. Did you ever play it when you used to ice skate? Everybody holds hands with the one in front of you and then everybody starts skating. When we're all skating fast, the leader turns quickly and sometimes the skaters at the end of the line fly off and sometimes land in a snow drift. I don't like to be at the end of the line! We always have a fire at the edge of the pond so we can warm up our feet. Sometimes we bring marshmallows to roast. Why do they always taste so much better if they're roasted over a fire? Anyway we had a lot of fun but by the time I got home I think my nose and cheeks were redder than any Santa Claus I've ever seen.

We're walking everywhere now since Daddy says we have to save the tires on our old car. Soon gasoline will be rationed if it isn't already.

Janie, Callie, and I were getting ready to play PIT when we looked out the window and saw Richard passing by. We went to the door and asked if he could come play. He came in and we had so much fun yelling "two for two" and "corner on wheat" or whatever. We were so noisy that Nana came in and asked what all the yelling was about. She also brought us chocolate chip cookies and a glass of milk. Yum! I hope they don't ration chocolate chip cookies!

I better get ready for bed since Daddy has told me that it's time at least twice!

I hope you are getting used to the rain. Maybe you'll get some snow one of these days.

Love, your cousin Patty

(*"I don't miss having a lot of snow now. Somehow driving in it isn't half as much fun as sliding down a hill on it!"*)

Mansfield, Oregon
February 2, 1942

Dear Patty,

I was so glad to get your letter. You can't believe how things have changed around here since the war. It isn't just having to have black shades to pull over the windows at night. Every conversation ends up with talk about the war.

Mama is taking classes at Linwood College so she can finish her degree. One of the teachers at the high school joined the army and the school board asked Mama to teach business and typing until the end of the year even if she doesn't have her degree yet.

She isn't sure what to do. She has time to go to school now because Daddy found a family to work the Yakimoto farm. Their name is McMinn and they have a sixteen-year-old son named Arlo and a six-year-old daughter named Imogene. They seem to be nice.

I still haven't told Mama about the present I got from Jackson., so it is still hidden in one of my drawers. I'm glad he didn't try to kiss me as Richard did you. I think I would just about die. We never see each other at school because the boys play baseball or football and we usually jump rope or play hop scotch. We eat at our desk in the classroom.

Margaret and I are still friends. Margaret's mother works as a bartender at the Log Palace. Since she works nights I am not allowed to spend much time at her house. She has three older brothers, two older sisters, and two younger sisters. It is a wild place to be. Her mom cooks lots of food during the day and the kids eat whenever they want to. They like that. Mama won't let us eat anything an hour before dinner because it will "spoil our appetite".

The kids don't talk about Sukie anymore. I guess they have forgotten her, but I haven't. I got a letter from her last week. She is still attending a school for Japanese children in Canada. She misses Oregon, but not the rain since there is as much rain there as here. I am glad she is there though, because President Roosevelt signed something called Japanese Internment. It means that Japanese-Americans will be sent to live in prison camps away from the coastline so they will not be able to signal Japanese planes and ships. This is what Sukie's father was afraid of. I asked Daddy if German-Americans will be sent away and he told me not to worry. But I worry anyway.

(Patty interrupted again. "Do you know what happened to Suki during the war?"

"Of course they weren't in the internment camps. The family became Canadian citizens. After the war

Suki went to college to become a teacher. She met her banker husband there. We met in Seattle once or twice and once Suki came here so she could see their old farm. I'm going to get in touch with her again.")

Mama and Daddy went to Portland to do some shopping. They really bought a lot of stuff like shoes and galoshes and sugar and toilet paper and fabric and kerosene for our camping lanterns. Mama said that some things will be hard to get so we need to stock up. The newspaper said some people are hoarding things that might be rationed like rubber galoshes. Galoshes are the ugliest boots you can imagine. Mama bought me some to fit now and a bigger size for next year. Lucky me! I'd just as soon they were rationed!

It usually doesn't get cold enough here for any ice skating so nobody has ice skates. Almost everyone has roller skates though and we have a roller rink where we play crack the whip too. From now on if I can't be close to the center I'm not going to play. Darlene was ahead of me and let go and the four of us were thrown against the wall. I'm still black and blue. I guess I'm a coward when it comes to danger!

I'm still praying that your parents will work things out. I hope you can come out here when school is out. Mama says we can pick strawberries and earn money to buy our own school clothes.

The weather report says we may get some snow this weekend. I can hardly wait.

I better close now and get to bed. This is a long letter!

Love, Carolyn

Wabash, Nebraska
February 20, 1942

Dear Carolyn,

I hope you got some snow, but since we've had lots of snow for three months already, it isn't too thrilling for me. I'll gladly send you some of ours! I'm getting tired of playing Fox and Geese at recess and I'm tired of watching out for the boys who want to throw snowballs at us when we walk home from school. We did have fun last weekend when we built a snow fort in our backyard. The boys came over and we chose sides and had a snow fight. Luckily the snow was pretty soft so nobody got hurt. I asked Nana if she'd make some chocolate chip cookies for us. She did and so we had cocoa and chocolate chip cookies after we got tired of the snowball fight.

I know what you mean about things being changed because of the war. We don't have to have blackout curtains here because we are so far from the oceans, but other things are different. There are little flags hanging from a lot of the windows. If they have a blue star on them, it means that someone in the family is in one of the services. If it is a gold star it means that someone in the family died fighting in the war. Luckily so far there aren't a lot of gold stars. Even the movies are different because every movie has a March of Time short first. It is always about the war. It usually comes before the cartoon and then comes the real movie. I don't like to watch the fighting.

Did your class have a Valentine's Day party? We did. We decorated a big box with valentines and red and pink crepe paper. It had a hole in the top so we could put our valentines in it. Callie and I spent one whole day doing our valentines. Daddy said we had to have a valentine for everybody in the classroom because we wouldn't want anybody to feel bad if they didn't get any. I tried to pick out one that fit each person and that's why it took so long. The funny ones I gave to the boys and the pretty ones to the girls. We all had fun opening the valentines at the party. It was so noisy that I expected teacher to yell at us, but she didn't. Lots of the valentines said "Guess who" where the name was supposed to be. I got a kind of lovey-dovey one and it said "guess who". I think it was from Richard because I saw him looking over at me when I opened it.

I was glad you remembered that Callie's birthday is on Valentine's Day. She was so happy to get your card and the dollar that was in it. Nana had a party for her. She invited all the girls in her class so there were twelve here plus Callie and me. I always wished my birthday was on Valentine's Day. It seems kind of special. Mama sent her a pretty new dress and a new Bobbsey Twins book. She sent me a pair of pink socks. I always get a little something on Callie's birthday and she gets something on mine. We may get to see Mama at Easter. We have Thursday, and Good Friday off so Daddy said maybe we can take the train to Omaha and visit Mama. I hope so. AND I hope I get to come out there after school is out. I'd love to earn money picking strawberries.

I wish we could send you some of our snow. You can have it!

Love, Patty

(Do they still have valentine day parties?" asked Patty. "My granddaughter's school has a 'winter' party now—not a Christmas party."

"Yes, but now they can't have any homemade treats. So much for homemade chocolate chip cookies. How sad!")

Mansfield, Oregon
March 1, 1942

Dear Patty,

We finally got some snow! It was so pretty. It covered the trees and bushes. We were glad it was Saturday so we didn't have to go to school. We ran out to play but it was so wet that our snowballs became ice balls. It all melted in one day. Margaret's mother said, "Spring snow is always mushy."

I bought a special valentine for Jackson. It said, "You are a special friend," and I signed it, "your friend, Carolyn." Isn't that a foolish a thing to do? We had one big valentine box just as you did. The party was mostly eating cookies, drinking punch, and passing out valentines. When the box was opened, the first thing out was a red heart box of chocolates from a "special friend"! I'm still being teased. "Who is Carolyn's special friend?" they all ask in a funny voice. I gave the box of chocolates to Mama from Jessie and me.

The movie, "Dumbo" finally came to town. I took Jessie to the matinee. Johnny and Jackson were there with their little brother, Calvin, so we all sat together. Jackson sat by me and Jessie kept grinning at us. She told Mama. Mama just said, "That was nice."

Jessie had to say, "Jackson loves Carolyn!"

Mama scolded her. Then Jessie said, "They held hands during the movie." I hit her and Mama sent us to our rooms to settle down. Mama came in later and said, "Jackson seems to be a nice boy but I don't think you should hold hands in movies."

We are invited to the MacIntosh farm for Easter. I am dreading it but I must admit it feels good to know that someone wants to be your boyfriend. Should I wear the locket he gave me?

I'm glad the McMinn family is on Suki's farm because now Jessie has a friend. She plays with Imogene all the time and doesn't follow me around so much anymore. Imogene, Jessie, and I gather eggs after school and clean them. Mrs. McMinn always has something good baked for us when we finish.

I'm glad that Mama decided not to teach this year. She wants to finish her degree.

Grandma and Grandpa Schmidt are moving here from Seattle so Messy Jessie and I have to share a bedroom. Grandma doesn't speak good English and she wants to teach us German. Mama says it is a good idea but not right now since we are at war with Germany. I agree with Mama. They'll be here by Easter so Jessie is moving in to my room today. Daddy is building bookshelves for us and Mama is covering boxes for us to keep things in. The room really looks nice but wait until Messy Jessie moves in with all her toys. Don't worry, there will be room for you if you come next summer because Daddy is going to fix up an empty room over the garage. It will even have its own bathroom. I wish it could be my room.

Write soon and tell me what to do about the locket.

Love, Carolyn

P.S. Is Richard still your boyfriend?

(Is Richard still your boyfriend! How many years were you married? 51?"

"No, fifty-three!" corrected Patty.)

Wabash, Nebraska
March 21, 1942

Dear Carolyn,

I'll answer your questions first. Number 1: Yes, wear the locket Jackson gave you. You don't have to tell anybody where it came from and there's no point in leaving it in your dresser. Number 2: No, I don't call Richard a boyfriend, but I like him best of the boys, I guess. He and Charles, Janie and Callie and I went out of town a mile or so, looking for scrap metal to turn in for the war effort. We collect it and take it where they say and then I think it is melted so they can make war machines out of it like tanks and jeeps and planes. We pulled three wagons and we found quite a few things that were lying in the ditches. We stopped at a couple of farm houses and they gave us some old metal things too. We are also saving all the foil from gum wrappers. We roll it into a ball and just keep adding foil to it. We are supposed to turn that in too. Nana is helping with the war effort. She saves the grease from the frying pans after she fries bacon or pork chops. She saves it in a big can and when it is full she takes it to the butcher and I think he turns it in somewhere. Somebody said they can make bombs from it.

We are lucky we are so far away from the war. When I see the fighting on the "March of Time" movie it scares me. They sometimes show the people that live where the fighting is and they always look so scared and worried.

The other night we saw a really scary movie. Richard and the other boys sat behind us and kept trying to scare us until the usher came and told them they would have to be quiet or leave. After that they didn't bother us. When the movie was over we were hoping they would walk home with us because Janie, Callie, and I were kind of scared to walk home. It is so dark on some of the streets. We were about half way home when those boys jumped out from behind a bush with a big yell. We were about scared to death! We are all mad at them. From now on we won't tell them when we're going to the movies so maybe they won't be there at the same time. That won't be easy because they always want to sit behind us and bother us.

Daddy said we can go visit Mama for Easter. Easter is early this year. It is on April fifth. We are getting to miss a couple of days of school. We'll go up on the train on Thursday and come home the Monday after Easter. We haven't seen Mama since Christmas so we are excited.

Have you and Jessie moved in together yet and are your grandparents there by now? I hope it won't be too bad having to share a room with your little sister. Callie and I have always had to share a room.

Write soon. Love, Patty

("Today we see wars on the national news every evening. and it's just as painful to watch now as it was then," said Patty.)

Mansfield, Oregon
April 20, 1942

Dear Patty,

Can you believe it! Our daffodils started blooming in February and now flowers are coming up everywhere. The fruit trees are blooming and the grass is so green. It's hard to be sad with everything so beautiful.

Our neighbor, Mrs. Robbins, told Mama that her brother was wounded somewhere in the Pacific. She doesn't know where it happened or any details because his letters were always censored. The official notice said he was on a hospital ship somewhere.

Daddy planted potatoes and onions in February. Imagine that! In Nebraska the ground would still be frozen. Mrs. Robbins told him when he should plant the peas, something about the dark of the moon or the light of the moon. How would the moon know? He'll plant the rest of the garden after the last frost. We always have a garden but now they are saying everybody should plant a Victory Garden. Are you going to plant one?

Mama was so busy she didn't have time to make our Easter outfits. She took Jessie and me into town and bought us each a hat, gloves, matching dresses, shoes, and a new slip to make the dress stand out. Mine is light blue and Jessie's is yellow.

Grandma and Grandpa Schmidt are living with us. Grandma does most of the cooking and cleaning so Mama has more time for school. We are learning to say both meal and bedtime prayers in German. Grandpa speaks English well and Daddy says Grandma understands it fairly well. Daddy says we have to be careful what we say around her. I've never seen Grandma smile. She doesn't want anyone to know that she can't speak English so I am trying to teach it to her. Grandpa is fun. He sings funny songs and plays cards with us. He takes care of the garden and helps Daddy with the farm.

Easter Sunday we went to a sunrise service at church. I was sleepy and Jessie fell asleep in Grandpa's lap. When we got home there were Easter baskets inside the screen porch. I know there's no Easter bunny so Mama or Daddy must have left them there, but Jessie thought the Easter bunny brought them. After breakfast Mama packed up the Easter breads, salads, and colored eggs and we went to the MacIntosh's. I wore the locket and Mama didn't say anything. Jackson smiled when he saw it. It rained all day so we played board games. After dinner we bigger kids got to hide the colored eggs for the little kids. We hid them in the basement. Calvin and Jessie were so excited.

I don't mind Jessie sharing my room even if she does have too many dolls and toys. I still like to play paper dolls so Jessie and I play that together. Sometimes I help her with her school work. I think I want to be a teacher someday.

Just a few weeks until school is out. I really hope you can come out and visit. Mrs. Robbins raises strawberries and said we can pick there. We'll get three cents a pound. She said the strawberries would start to ripen the last week in May. Mama is going to ask your mom and dad if you can come. Maybe your Mom can come and visit too. Beg if you have to, but be sure to come!

Love, Carolyn

Wabash, Nebraska
May 7, 1942

Dear Carolyn,

Mama says I can come out to Oregon and pick strawberries with you. I'm so excited!

She said she'll come with me. Nana is going to take Callie to Chicago while I'm gone.

They are going to visit Nana's sister, Aunt Adele. I got to go there with Nana when I was little. I loved all the lights in Chicago and I especially loved Chinatown. We had tea there and Aunt Adele bought me some funny light colored candy. I have never seen it around here. Nana bought me a little Chinese doll that had a squeakier in it's stomach. I think I still have it somewhere in my room.

Anyway, I'm so glad I get to come see you. Mama said we can stay ten days and then we have to come back because she can't miss any more work. We can have a lot of fun in ten days, can't we?

Callie and I went to Mama's for Easter. The train was packed with soldiers and sailors. They got to get on the train first but then they let us on because the conductor said he would watch out for us and be sure we got off in Omaha. Some of the soldiers started singing and Callie and I sang along too. I liked "Don't Sit Under the Apple Tree With Anyone Else but Me," and "Praise the Lord and Pass the Ammunition" the best.

Mama was waiting for us when we got to Omaha. She looked cute in a red corduroy skirt and jacket and a little red jockey hat. The soldiers whistled at her! She blushed and waved at them. We had Easter dinner at Grandma's. I tried to play their piano but it was so damaged in the Carter Lake flood that it won't play much anymore. After dinner we all played games. I'm glad all the grown-ups in our family like to play games. This time we played Monopoly. It's good practice for Callie counting up all that money all the time. Grandma won. Callie and I were partners and we had Park Place and Boardwalk so we thought we would win, but I kept landing on Illinois Avenue and it was expensive with three houses on it!

Just think, less than a month, and I'll be visiting you! I can't wait!

Love, Patty

("You know that Monopoly set that we played with was made by Mama and her sisters. They couldn't afford to buy a set when they were girls. I still have it. Did your mom ever tell you about it?"

"Yes, she did. I'd love to see it sometime. We really lived through an amazing time, didn't we?")

Mansfield, Oregon
May 21, 1942

Dear Patty,

I'm so excited for you to come. I can't wait for May 31st when you'll get here. Daddy is saving his gas so we can go to Portland and get you and then we'll all take a trip to the ocean. The strawberries are beginning to ripen. We should be able to start picking on Monday, the day after you get here. Our school is out the last Thursday in May unless the farmers need the kids to pick the strawberries earlier. I don't think we'll get out early this year because Daddy brought in some berries from our garden and they were still so sour that they needed a lot of sugar.

Mansfield had a tulip festival last week. There was a big parade Saturday. The boy scouts carried the big flags of Oregon and the United States. Jackson really looks cute in a uniform even if it is just a boy scout one. We girl scouts carried small flags. We did a formation where we pivoted and also did crossovers. Mama said we looked good but we really got mixed up there for awhile. After the parade there was a carnival in the park. There were no carnival rides. It was just food booths and pitching pennies at bottles. I pitched three pennies without hitting a dish. I was just ready to quit when I decided to pitch onemore. I got the penny in a dish and won a covered glass candy dish. Mama uses it for jelly because we hardly ever have any candy.

Troop trains come from Fort Lewis, Washington on their way to Camp Adair. Jessie has a Red Cross nurse's uniform that she loves to wear. As the train passed one day, she saluted. I was just waving, but the soldiers yelled and cheered and saluted back. They even threw coins out the window. Jessie and I gathered over a dollar in pennies and nickels and dimes. Mama was upset with us but Daddy laughed and thought it was great.

We are saving tin cans like you are to help with the war. I have to take the labels off of the cans and open both ends. Then I step on them so that they are flat. Daddy takes them and drops them off at the train depot. To help save food, everyone in Mansfield cans everything. Daddy planted a huge garden and Mama bought a bunch of canning jars at the church rummage sale so she will be able to can all the things that he grows in his victory garden.

Stay healthy. I don't want anything to happen so you can't come.

Love, Carolyn

("Nothing tastes better than fresh vegetables from the garden," said Patty. "The best I can do these days are some cherry tomatoes in half a large wine barrel.")

Wabash, Nebraska
June 30, 1942

Dear Carolyn,

Mama always says to be sure to write a thank you letter when you visit someone so I'm writing one. I would want to anyway since I had such a GREAT time! Thank you and your mama and daddy for inviting Mama and me. I saw so much and learned so much but best of all, had SO much FUN!

I loved the strawberry picking—well, I loved getting the money and I loved some of it. I didn't really love getting covered with sticky strawberry juice and then the dust turning it into mud. But I did love eating the strawberries. Here at home strawberries are expensive and we usually just get enough to have strawberry shortcake once or twice. But in those fields we could eat as many as we wanted to and I ate a LOT. The first night I was sick to my stomach from eating so many. Then I can't really say I enjoyed getting hit in the head by a strawberry, thrown by who know who. Whenever the row boss asked who was throwing them, everybody was innocent, of course. We were pretty bad at picking those strawberries at first. Remember how many times the row boss made us go back and clean up our row? But by the time the week was over, we were pretty good at it! I didn't love getting up at five in the morning to walk to the Robbins' strawberry field, but I sure loved going to the swimming pool afterward. That swimming pool lady was really mean about being sure we got all that strawberry gunk off of us. She wouldn't even let us go in the pool if we had a little under our fingernails. But didn't that water feel great after it had been so hot in the fields? I'm glad they let us go home at two o'clock. And now I have fifty dollars to buy new school clothes. I've never had so much money before! Daddy says we can go to Omaha and Mama can take us shopping before school starts.

I know Mama had a good time too. She misses your mama. Being twins, they used to talk to each other every day and now they can't. I thought they would talk all night every night.

And as for Jackson, he is cute. I think he looks a little bit like Mickey Rooney.

Freckles are cute on boys, but I don't like them on me!

I'm glad your daddy took us to Salem. Now I can tell my sixth grade teacher that I went through the Oregon capital. It looks a lot like Nebraska's capital. Daddy took us through that once. We sat in on a session when Wendell Wilkie was talking. You know, the one who ran for president but he lost.

Anyway thank you for a wonderful time. Maybe you can come here next summer and visit me. We don't have any way to earn money since kids can't pick corn but we can have fun, sitting on Janie's porch and seeing who can spit the farthest. Ha, ha!

Love, Patty

(Carolyn laughed and said," I think the only thing Mama and Daddy ever fought over was the huge phone bills from Mama talking to your mama.")

Mansfield, Oregon
July 15, 1942

Dear Patty,

It is so lonely here since you left. I really miss you. I wish you could have stayed until after the 4th of July because Uncle Klaus and Aunt Maude rented a huge house at the ocean west of Tillamook. There was a boat dock and we caught lots of salmon. We dug clams and bought oysters. Everything was so delicious. We cooked everything on a fire on the beach. We had to have the fire out by sundown because of the blackout. We stayed on the beach all afternoon.

Jessie found a strange looking metal object. We keep hearing that the Japanese are sending mines to America on the Japanese current. We reported the object to the beach patrol and they called the coast guard. They made everybody stand back. Then they took the object away. Uncle Klaus thinks it was part of a boat engine but we have to report anything unusual.

I told Mama that I hoped one of the bombs would blow up a Japanese ship but Mama said, "You better pray that none of the bombs explode anywhere."

Did you hear that a Japanese submarine fired on Fort Stevens? Fort Stevens is just a few miles north of where we stayed. That happened on June 29th and we got here on July 3rd. Many people sit on the hillsides and watch for Japanese subs with binoculars. Rumors of a Japanese invasion are everywhere. Sometimes I am scared but Daddy says to not worry. Mama has volunteered to watch for Japanese planes at a lookout station west of Mansfield. The lookout station has posters of Japanese and also American planes on the walls. When a plane is identified it is recorded on a sheet of paper. If the plane is not an American plane the report is called in and American planes scramble to search for it.

I feel so patriotic these days. My eyes tear-up whenever I see an American flag or hear the national anthem.

Write soon,

Love, Carolyn

("We could not even imagine then that people would disrespect the flag the way some have done."

"I know what you mean," said Patty. "Do you remember when I came out to visit and we went to Fort Stevens and saw the bunkers from the 2nd World War? They seemed so little")

Wabash, Nebraska
August 10, 1942

Dear Carolyn,

My goodness! Things are really exciting where you live. The newsreels are about all we see here that are exciting. Well, we see stars in the windows to show that someone in that house has gone to war and we see posters around. One of the posters says, "Loose lips, sink ships." Daddy says that means we aren't to talk about things that might help the enemy. I don't know anything that might help the enemy but I think I won't tell anybody about what you told me about the firing on Fort Stevens. Maybe that is something I shouldn't talk about. It's okay for you and me to talk about it though.

I know what you mean about feeling patriotic. I always get tears in my eyes when I see the flag or hear the national anthem. *"I guess this time may have been the last time when it seemed like the entire country was together. The Republicans and the Democrats tried to work together to win the war, not like today where they argue about everything!)*

The other day Janie, Callie, Richard and George and I decided to try to get some more metal for the scrap drive. We took the three wagons and went out to the other side of town to see if we could find any. A couple of houses had some old bottle caps to give us and one lady gave us a pipe that had come off their car and was too rusted to fix. Maybe we got enough to help a little bit. We were tired so Richard and George said they'd take it and leave it at the scrap metal collecting place. We stopped at Janie's and were sitting on her porch when they got back. It was too hot to play Andy, Andy, Over so we went down in Janie's basement and played Monopoly. Richard won again! Next time I'm not going to let him buy even one of my properties.

Have you spent your picking money yet? Daddy used up almost all of his gas ration taking us to Omaha so Mama could help us pick out a few new clothes for school. Mama had made Callie and me a skirt and jacket out of a pink tweed. I think they are cute but WAY too hot for August. She took us to Carter Lake so we could go swimming. I don't really know how to swim so we just fooled around in the shallow water. All of a sudden everybody was running up the bank. A boy had been pulled out of the water. He had drowned. Oh, Carolyn, he looked so pale. I felt so bad that I didn't want to swim anymore so we went back to Mama's place.

Daddy came and got us on Sunday afternoon. He's getting ready for school too. He's writing lesson plans already.

Be careful out there in Oregon. Maybe your family should move back to Nebraska. I wish you would!

Love, Patty

("Did you ever learn to swim?" asked Carolyn.

"Not really," said Patty. "I had to learn in college but I'm still not good at it!")

Mansfield, Oregon
September 15, 1942

Dear Patty,

I was so glad to open our mailbox and find a letter from you waiting for me. Be glad you live in Nebraska. Oregon is so beautiful but it is close to the Pacific Ocean and closer to Japan. A place in southern Oregon was bombed last week. The bomb landed near Mt. Emily, but no damage was done.

(Carolyn laughed. "We didn't know it then, but an unmarked Japanese submarine brought an unassembled plane all the way from Japan. Then when they were near our coast, they emerged and assembled the plane on their deck, intending that the pilot start a fire near Mt. Emily. The pilot had two bombs in the cockpit with him and had to drop them

by hand. The first one was a dud and the second one landed so near a ranger station that the rangers were quickly able to put the fire out and so there was no damage to speak of. It amazes me how they kept it out of the papers!"

"That doesn't happen now," said Patty. "Everything is for public knowledge now, both truth and lies!"

Carolyn nodded, picked up the letter and continued reading.)

I went with Mama to watch for aircraft. It is exciting but really scary. Daddy told me that I can't tell Jessie anymore war stories. She is having bad dreams and climbs in bed with them every night.

I wish you could have been here when we drove to Silver Creek Falls for the Nebraska picnic. There were acres and acres of beautiful blue flowers. Daddy said that the blue flowers are flax. Linen is made from flax. Oregon has the perfect climate for it. The linen is being used to make parachutes because it is hard to get silk anymore. Because so many men are in the service, convicts from the prison are being used to harvest it.

Mama, Daddy, Jessie, and I went out and picked beans on the weekend to help with the war effort. A bus picked us up and drove us to the bean field. Jessie and I each got half of what our family earned. We are to buy school clothes and school workbooks with it. In Oregon we have to buy our own workbooks. The rest of the money we used to buy war bonds. Daddy is in charge of the bond drive for Mansfield. I guess he wants us to set a good patriotic example.

I'm glad you and Richard are still good friends. School has started here and Jackson and Johnny are in the room next to mine so we have to share a coat closet. Jackson and I don't talk much to each other because we don't want to be teased. We are both in the school chorus and are practicing for a school program. We are singing, "We Did It Before and We Can Do It Again" and "The White Cliffs of Dover." We are learning a march that goes with these two songs.

Remember the pile of junk scrap metal that covered the courthouse lawn when we went to visit the Salem capital? Of course it was for the war effort but you should see it now! Some artists and welders are making it into a statue that has moving parts. They call it Scrappo. It wasn't finished when we saw it but we saw a picture of it in the Salem paper. It is becoming famous. Scrappo's jaw moves and a ventriloquist speaks for it. It's going to be on the newsreels so watch for it.

It must have been awful for you to see that poor boy who drowned. I think about all the people in Europe and China who have bombs dropping on them every day. On the way to school we see a house with a gold star in the window. It makes me so sad to think someone in that house had someone they loved die in the war.

We are going to Uncle Klaus and Aunt Maude's farm this weekend. Their truck has broken down and they can't even buy parts for it because all the auto factories are making war machines. Daddy is looking in junkyards to see if he can find parts for the truck.

I miss you, Patty, and wish you were here.

Love, Carolyn

("We later learned that Italian and German prisoners of war from Camp Adair were used to help make linen and help with other farm labor," said Carolyn)

"I remember prisoners of war serving in the officer's club in Georgia where my stepfather was stationed," added Patty.)

Wabash, Nebraska
October 20, 1942

Dear Carolyn,

It must be exciting to live on the coast, but maybe it is a little scary too. Not too much happens here but we know there is a war because so many of the men are in the services. Most of them around here are in the army but some are in the air force, the navy, or the coast guard. I've learned all the songs from the different services except the coast guard one. I haven't heard that much. I like "Anchors Aweigh" the best.

Janie's big brother came home on leave last week. He couldn't tell us where he'll be sent. He said that he isn't sure where he is going. He is a corporal now and looked so nice in his uniform. Janie cried when he had to leave again.

At school we're having a contest to see which room can buy the most war savings stamps. Every Friday we bring our money and buy as many as we can. There are books of ten cent stamps and books of twenty-five cent stamps. Callie and I are trying to fill ten cent ones. Right now the fourth grade class is a little bit ahead but the contest isn't over until the end of April so we have time to catch up. I'm trying to think of a way to earn some money so I can buy more of the stamps. The radio stations are always saying that everybody can help in the war effort and that's one way we can help. I heard about selling the "Grit" magazine and Nana said that if Callie and I can go together, we can try to sell it. I don't like to sell things very much but we might try it. Callie is better at it so maybe she'll do the talking.

Janie told me that Miss Darby is dating Daddy. I like her but I hope that is not true because I'm still hoping Mama will come home again. Miss Darby plays the piano for Sunday School sometimes. I think she works for the draft board. They decide who has to go into the service and who needs to stay home, either because they are too old or not well or are doing work for the war effort. Of course I'm not glad that Daddy is 4F because he is blind in one eye, but since it kept him out of the service and at home with us, I'm thankful about that.

I'm not going to have a Halloween party this year. There is going to be one at the church and that will be enough.

Richard and Charles came over last night. It was cold but not so cold that it was snowing, so we played Kick the Can. Callie and Janie played too. It was really dark so the one who was "It" had a hard time finding any of us. Richard and I were hiding in the bushes on the other side of the garage when Nana called me to come in and practice my piano lessons. The rest of them got to play for another half hour. It was beginning to feel like snow so we probably won't be able to play Kick the Can much longer.

Tell Jackson and his brother "Hi" for me. It was nice to get to know your friends when I was out there in the strawberry fields with you.

Take care of yourself!

Love, Patty

("Neighborhood games were such fun! We played kick the can, hide and seek and kickball.

I feel sorry for kids today who are obsessed with computer games. They miss so much!"

"Yes," agreed Patty. "We never had any problem with obesity between the games and walking everywhere we went.")

Mansfield, Oregon
November 15, 1942

Dear Patty,

I think I told you that Mama was watching for Japanese aircraft. She is an official spotter for the Oregon Aircraft Warning Service. It is like the system the English people use to watch the skies and seas for German planes and boats. She was told that observers must be more careful now because of General Doolittle's raid on Japan. The Japanese are likely to want to get back at us. Mama and Mrs. Robbins work together at the lookout. While they are there they make quilts because most of the time there is nothing happening.

I didn't tell Mama about Uncle Don and Miss Darby. She still hopes that your dad and mom will get back together.

Jackson and Johnny are playing junior varsity basketball. It's unusual for seventh graders to be on the team but Jackson and Johnny are really good. All their games are in the daytime because car lights are not allowed after dark. The only time I get to watch them is when they have home games. Our teacher excuses the ones who want to watch, but she makes us do all the work that we miss. Margaret and I always go to the games even if it makes more homework that night.

Thanksgiving will be at our house this year because Aunt Maude is going to have a baby in May. They have been married for fifteen years and they had given up on ever having any children. Aunt Maude wants to be careful so she doesn't think she could do all the cooking for Thanksgiving this year. Grandpa and Grandma are staying with them to help with the farm and housework but Jessie won't move out of my room anyway.

Daddy brought two huge turkeys home for Thanksgiving dinner. We are feeding them corn to fatten them up. Jessie named one of them Shirley after her favorite movie star, Shirley Temple. I named the other one Grumpy because she chases me when I feed her. Catastrophe struck this morning because when Daddy went out to kill them for Thanksgiving dinner, Shirley was gone. Grumpy was still there but no Shirley. Daddy asked Jessie if she knew where Shirley was. Jessie would not answer him. We don't know if she hid Shirley or if she turned her loose out in the woods. Even if there is only one turkey tomorrow, there will be plenty for dinner and maybe for leftovers.

Every Monday we buy war stamps at our school just as you do. The class that buys the most stamps before Washington's birthday on February 22nd, will get a free ice cream party from the local creamery. What is your prize for the winning class? I hope you win and I hope we win too.

Are you going to your mama's in Omaha for Thanksgiving?

Write soon.

Love, Carolyn

("Oh, yes, I remember that Shirley story!" laughed Patty.)

Wabash, Nebraska
December 15, 1942

Dear Carolyn,

I bet Jessie hid Shirley somewhere. Did you ever find her and did you get to keep her as a pet?

I hope you win the war stamp sale prize too. The winner of our stamp contest gets to go spend a whole day seeing "Gone With the Wind" at the Bijou. That will be so much fun. It is such a long movie that we are going to see half of it in the morning and then go home for lunch and see the other half in the afternoon. Did you see that I said "we"? Of course I don't know that it will be us but I think sixth graders would like a movie like "Gone With the Wind" more than fourth or fifth graders. The fourth graders probably wouldn't even understand it. Right now the fifth graders have bought the most stamps but we aren't giving up. Our contest lasts until the first of April.

Everything looks like Christmas around here. We haven't put the tree up yet because Daddy says it will dry out. We're going to do it this Saturday. We have our little red wreath up in the window though. Callie and I went downtown to the dime store after school yesterday to see what we might be able to buy Mama and Daddy and Nana. Nana likes us to make her something so I am knitting her a pot holder. I have to do it shut up in our play room so she won't see me. Callie is making something at school for her. I think it is a bread board like I made in school last year. I had some yarn left so I didn't have to buy any. I think we are going to get Mama some Blue Waltz perfume again. It doesn't smell as good as Evening in Paris but I don't think we have enough money for that. We may get Daddy a new tie or maybe a new pen. I think we'll go after school on Friday and buy the things so we can wrap them.

It snowed yesterday so they closed the street by the school so we kids could sled on it. We went up there right after school and sledded until it began to get dark. Richard pulled my sled up the hill for me most of the time. By the time we got home our cheeks and noses were as red as can be. Nana had supper ready. It was beef stew. There wasn't much beef in it because our meat ration stamps are getting low, but it was good because Nana is a good cook. She still had apples from the tree in the back so she'd made an apple cobbler.

Do you go with your mom to watch out for enemy planes very often? I don't think we have to worry about that. We are in the middle of the country so German planes would have to fly a long way west to get here and Japanese planes a long way east. We don't even have blackouts at night. But we do have a lot of people in the armed service and all of us are trying to help by saving grease, metal, etc. I have a big ball of aluminum foil that I've saved from gum. I'll turn it in soon. Someone told me that in North Platte the women meet all the trains and give the servicemen on the train doughnuts and other things. I don't think the trains that stop here have many servicemen on them.

I wish you were going to be here for Christmas. I'm going to stick this letter in a Christmas card we made at school.

Write soon.

Love, Patty

Mansfield, Oregon
December 31, 1942

Dear Patty,

I was glad to get your letter. I loved the Christmas card you made. It's still on my bulletin board. I miss Nebraska's blue skies and snow. It has rained for days now and even if it isn't raining, the air is damp and cold. We leave the lights on inside all day if we have to read or sew. It gets dark by five-thirty daylight savings time. Daddy never gets to see the outside of the house during daylight since he leaves for work by 6:30 and doesn't get home until 6 at night.

Since you asked, I'll tell you the fate of Jessie's turkey, Shirley. Well, Jessie now has a pet turkey. She won't tell us where she hid her, but I think she brought Shirley to our neighbor's old chicken coop. It hadn't been used in years until last summer when we cleaned it out for a play house. Shirley is now terrorizing the hens in our chicken yard. Daddy says if the egg production goes down, Shirley may not be here long.

You asked if I go with Mama to watch for enemy aircraft on Saturdays. We HAVE to go if Daddy has to work even though I really think I'm old enough to stay home with Jessie. It is boring our there because Jessie and I don't get to do anything but read or draw.

We had a nice Christmas. We got our tree from the woods behind our house.

That's something we never got to do in Nebraska. It's fun to pick one out and then have Daddy cut it down. It looked really pretty and we "frosted" it again.

For Christmas I got three Nancy Drew mysteries and two Louisa May Alcott books and a hand-knit blue sweater with white snowflakes made by Grandma Schmidt. It is beautiful. I can hardly wait for school to start again so I can wear it. Mama fixed a turkey dinner. We eat a lot of turkey out here but not Shirley—yet!

(Carolyn stopped and laughed. "Jessie didn't like it, but Shirley had to go back to Uncle Klaus's farm because she kept jumping on the hens' nests and breaking the eggs. We don't know what happened to her after she went there." She picked up her letters and began again.)

I know our class is going to win the war savings stamp contest and get the ice cream party because six of us sixth-graders have decided to each spend five dollars of our summer picking money to buy stamps. We are going to wait to buy them until just before the contest ends. We aren't going to tell anyone because we don't want anyone else to get the same idea. I hope the party will be during math class. Math isn't hard but why do we have to add columns with numbers in the ten millions? It's just the same as adding hundreds but easier to make a mistake. I like story problems but I hate adding those columns.

It's eleven thirty p.m. and I'm really sleepy, but I want to stay up long enough to see 1943 come in.

Write soon.

Love, Carolyn

P.S. It's 12:01 January 1, 1943. I made it! Happy New Year!

(Carolyn put the letter down and said, "I don't know about you, but I'm getting hungry. Let's go to that good restaurant that we ate at once when we were here. You remember—I think it was called Grandma Tilley's Diner."

"That place is long gone! There's a McDonald's on that block now. Do you feel like fast food?"

"No, I want somebody to wait on me and bring me a tall glass of iced tea."

It was late afternoon before they returned to the hotel and picked up the letters again.

"I guess my letter is next," Patty said. "It's dated January 15, 1943".)

Wabash, Nebraska
January 15, 1943

Dear Carolyn,

Happy New Year to you too! I'm glad you made it this year. I guess you could say I did too. I got to see the hands of the clock past midnight but I really wasn't awake the whole time. I was reading one of my old books, "Emily Climbs" by the same author as "Anne of Green Gables" and I fell asleep about ten o'clock. All of a sudden I heard a loud noise and it woke me up. I ran to the window and saw a bunch of people at Aldrich's house across the street. They were banging on pots and yelling "It's almost here!" (I think they had too much to drink!) Anyway it was 11:55 so I waited another five minutes and saw the new year come in. Wouldn't it be great if 1943 was the year the war ended? I hope it is. We had a nice Christmas too. Mama didn't come this year but since we had two weeks off from school, Callie and I got to ride the train to Omaha to visit her. I guess the only good thing about Mama and Daddy not being together anymore is that we had two Christmas days. I'd still rather have them together! I got a pair of figure skates from Daddy. I guess he and Mama must have talked about it because she gave me a skating outfit. It has a cute short skirt and a darling jacket to match. Callie got the same thing except mine is green tweed and hers is pink. I hope we have nerve enough to wear them at the pond. I'm not a good enough skater to wear an outfit and I'm afraid the kids will think we're showing off if we have an entire special skating outfit to wear!

In Omaha we got to go to the Orpheum and see both a show and a stage show. The stage show had Wee Bonnie Baker in it. She sang "Oh, Johnny." I try to sing like her in a high little girl voice. Callie laughs at me and then she tries it and I laugh at her. We got to spend some time at Grandma's house too. She has a lot of old books that I read.

When we got home I went over to Janie's and we decided to go out and build a big snowman since the snow was just right. We had just gotten started when Richard and Charles came by. They wanted to have a snowball fight so Janie let them go in the house and call a few friends. We chose up sides. Richard chose me. I wanted Janie on our side but Charles picked her first! Then we built a fort. We worked fast so we had time to make a pile of snowballs before the fight started. The snowballs were soft so nobody got hurt. We thought we were winning but all of a sudden Charles and two or three others came from behind us and got us! They had sneaked around Janie's house and surprised us. Afterwards I ran home and asked Nana if everybody could come over for cocoa and leftover Christmas cookies and she said okay. Yummy!

Now all the fun is over and school is on again. Nothing new there. We are really getting pretty good at singing parts in music class. I'm glad I get to sing alto. It's fun to sing harmony.

Daddy's calling me for supper so I better stop!

Love, Patty

(Patty paused and said, "Learning harmony was one of the best things I ever did. I've enjoyed singing in school and church choirs all my life!")

Mansfield, Oregon
February 10, 1943

Dear Patty,

Mama, Jessie, and I went with Daddy to Portland last week. Daddy got extra gas rations because he had to negotiate a lumber sale at a place called Kaiserville. Daddy says Kaiserville is a mess. It is now the second largest city in Oregon. Houses there are being built for over 100,000 people who have come to Oregon to build ships for the navy. It is huge! The official sign going into Kaiserville says Vanport which is a combination of Vancouver, Washington and Portland, Oregon. Most people still call it Kaiserville and aren't very happy about it being built. I heard it was built next to Portland instead of inside of it because only white people are allowed to live inside Portland. I wonder why.

When we were downtown shopping we saw a lot of Negroes. I don't think I ever saw one in Nebraska except in the movies. I guess I was staring because one girl saw me gawking and she stuck out her tongue. I smiled and waved at her and she smiled and waved back. I asked Mama about this but she said we'd talk later. Later all she said was that these were strange times. I think she didn't know what to say.

*("We still have a ways to go on civil rights,"
interrupted Patty, "but how far we have come since
that time."*

*"Right," agreed Carolyn. "The black community
finally got to move to Portland when the Columbia
River flooded and washed the entire city of Vanport
away in 1948."*

*"Oh, I kind of remember you telling about that. At
least something good came out of that flood.")*

Mama got a letter from Suki's mom. She said
that the tea bushes she had planted before they left,
should be about ready to harvest. She's going to tell
Mama how to harvest and dry it. Then we can share
the tea. Mama thinks that we can harvest enough
tea to send some to Aunt Opal.

Uncle Klaus bought a junkyard and he is gathering
repair parts for trucks. It is hard for farmers to get
crops to the market now because the farm trucks
are wearing out and all the new parts go to the
military. He has sold most of the scrap metal to a
place in Portland. He is rebuilding truck parts in
his shop.

Margaret and I are on the committee to plan the
Valentine's Day party. Margaret wants to have a
dance but I think the teacher won't allow it and I don't
want her to think it was my idea. I like Margaret but

Margaret doesn't like it when people disagree with her. I don't know what to do What would you do?

Write soon.

Love, Carolyn

Wabash, Nebraska
March 3, 1943

Dear Carolyn,

I think you shouldn't let Margaret have her own way all the time. If she gets mad at you, so what! She'll forget it in no time.

There are so many exciting things happening out in Oregon. Here in Wabash things seem almost the same as before the war except for all the rationing. We walk everywhere because we don't have any gas to go anywhere and Nana is always telling us to be careful with our shoes because we may not be able to get some new ones because of rationing.

It is still cold here. I can't wait for the snow to melt now. I love it when it first comes but now I'm tired of it. I'm tired of snowball fights, sledding down the school hill, and Fox and Geese at recess! I'm even tired of skating at the brickyard pond. It's time for spring!

We had the usual valentine's day party at school. Nana and Janie's mother sent cupcakes. I got another "secret" valentine. It was a really pretty one. I just know it was from Richard but since it said "Guess Who" on it, I couldn't tell him thank you for it.

We are a little ahead in the war savings stamps contest. I sure hope we win. Callie and I sold ten Grit magazines and got a little money from that but Daddy said we couldn't go out selling anymore. It is too cold and gets dark too early, so we need to find another way to get money for the stamps.

Callie's birthday was on Valentine's day and she had a party. All the girls in her class came over. They played games and had cake and ice cream. Mama sent her a darling new dress. She sent me a dollar and I used it for savings stamps. Daddy gave Callie a book she likes. It was a new Bobbsey Twin book. He also gave her a Monopoly game. We had fun playing it with him after the party.

Do you remember Esther who is in my class at school? Her big brother was killed somewhere in a battle in the Pacific. We felt so sorry for her. She started crying at recess and we came inside with her and talked. She has one other brother who is in high school and she is afraid he will have to go to war too.

Our family has only Uncle Phil in the service. He is a cook in a camp in Kansas. He has flat feet so he didn't think he would be drafted but he was. I guess they think it's okay to have flat feet if you are a cook. You remember Uncle Phil? He still has that old model A Ford that he loves to drive when he comes home on leave. He said it can turn on a dime.

When you come back to Nebraska to visit, we'll have to go see all the relatives and that means Uncle Phil if the war is over by then.

Time for bed if I want to have time to read for awhile.

Love, Patty

(Carolyn said, "I still have some sugar rationing stamps that Mama saved. I didn't even know that children were issued the rationing stamps in their own name until Mama gave me mine a few years ago."

"I wish I had some of those old rationing stamps but I don't," said Patty.)

Mansfield, Oregon
April 15, 1943

Dear Patty,

I'm so glad it is spring here. I love Oregon for its beautiful and early spring. Grandma and Grandpa Schmidt are staying with us for a few weeks again. Grandma and the women's group at church are knitting stump socks for the wounded soldiers. They are for soldiers who have lost an arm or a leg. Jessie and I are learning to knit so we can help. I am also knitting a red, white, and blue cap. It is the same pattern.

Do you use oleomargarine in Nebraska? We make our own butter here but Mama is mixing oleomargarine with it to make it go farther. Grandma Schmidt doesn't like that one bit. She shakes her head and says, "Nein! Nein!" I think she speaks German just to annoy Mama. We don't have to worry about the butter being rationed because we make our own but the more we use the less cream we can sell. And the more cream we sell the more money we make.

Grandma is making Easter outfits for Jessie and me. Thank goodness they aren't alike this year. Mine is made princess style with plain elbow-length sleeves. Jessie's dress is yellow and has ruffles and cap sleeves. I love Jessie but I'm too old for ruffles.

Our school had a memorial service for Mr.Carlson. He was the seventh grade teacher last year but he was drafted so he joined the navy. His ship was sunk by the Japanese. After the service some of the girls asked me if I still hear from Sukie. I don't know if I am ashamed that I am still friends with her or not, but I just said, "No." I really haven't heard from her for a long time so I wasn't really lying. Mama still keeps in touch with their family so I know Suki is okay.

("You know I've always felt guilty about not telling those girls that I still kept in touch with Suki.")

I'm so excited! Mama says that Jessie and I can come and visit you the first two weeks in July. She hopes she can come too but if she can't Jessie and I will come alone on the bus. I can't wait to see you and Callie and Grandma and Aunt Opal!

Love, Carolyn

Wabash, Nebraska
May 7, 1943

Dear Carolyn,

I'm already excited at the thought that you might get to come and stay with us awhile this summer. I'm going to start thinking of things to do just in case you do come.

We don't have a beach to go to and there isn't any picking for us to do to make money so I'll have to think hard.

The most exciting thing that has happened is that the sixth grade did win the war savings stamp contest. We had an assembly and the principal congratulated us and said we would be going to "Gone With The Wind" on April 16th as our prize. We had to clap and yell a little but the teacher shushed us right away.

I really liked the movie. Have you seen it? I didn't like the war part where all the wounded were lying around and the women were trying to help them. I also didn't like it when Scarlett and Rhett's little girl, Bonnie, died. I was crying but I didn't let anybody see me. Clark Gable is so handsome that I don't see how Scarlett could have liked Ashley Wilkes better than him. It ended with Rhett leaving and saying he didn't give a "damn", which shocked all of us. I am going to rewrite the ending and have Rhett come back after Scarlett turns into a nicer person and begs him to come. They can rebuild Tara and have another little girl. I like happy endings!

We got two other days off in April because we always get the Thursday and Friday before Easter off. Easter was the 25th this year. That is kind of late. Callie and I still hunted for Easter eggs even though of course we know there isn't an Easter bunny. In fact, we not only hunted them, but we dyed them ourselves and then I hid some eggs for Callie in the front yard (I didn't want to hunt them in the front yard in case Richard or somebody would see me doing that kiddy thing!) and she hid mine in the backyard. Then we went to Sunday School. We stayed for church with Nana since it was Easter. I didn't get a new dress this year but I did get a new pair of shoes and so did Callie. It was lucky we had enough ration stamps to get them since both of us were growing out of our old ones. Mama sent us each a pretty new hat to wear to church. Of course mine was blue and Callie's pink. That's the way it always is. When I grow up I'm only going to buy pink things for myself.

Only another week and a half of school. We get out on the nineteenth this year. The bigger boys need to get out to help with the crops. Some of them will get out even a little earlier to help since so many men are away in the service. I wish I could help in the fields. We are going to have a victory garden though. Daddy bought some seeds—corn, tomatoes, carrots, lettuce, radishes, and beets. We are pulling out all the old flowers from last summer and Daddy is going to dig up the ground so we can start planting.

Oh, I just about forgot to answer your questions. Yes, we use oleomargarine here and I don't like it. I don't like to mix the coloring in it either.

My favorite actor is Van Johnson. I think he is so cute! Who do you like?

I can't wait until you get here!

Love, Patty

Mansfield, Oregon
June 20, 1943

Dear Patty,

Exciting news! Aunt Maude and Uncle Klaus have a beautiful baby boy named James Joseph. He is adorable and Aunt Maude lets us hold him. Grandma Schmidt hovers over us and sings in German while we hold little Jimmy. I thinks she annoys Aunt Maude as much as she annoys Mama, but I'm just a kid so what do I know!

I have just finished packing and can hardly believe that I will see you in less than a week. I helped Jessie get organized. She is as excited as I am. Neither of us have ever ridden on a bus that far before. Mama is bringing a bag of apples to snack on but we will be eating at bus stops. We will be there on July 3rd. I feel like I'm coming home and I think Mama does too.

Daddy bought a freezer from a junk dealer and he is cleaning it up. It was once in an ice cream parlor that has gone out of business. It looks really nifty on our back porch. Ha, ha!

Mama is bringing some of our tea leaves for Aunt Opal. She is afraid that we may have picked them too early for black tea. I drink tea now. I am not sure I like it but Grandma Schmidt said I would acquire a taste for it. She puts milk and sugar in it so it is too sweet for me.

I have a new pen pal. Our class had a new project to write to local people who are in the armed service. We didn't know who would get our letter or if they would answer back. I got a letter back from a navy nurse named, Betty Bell. She used to live in Mansfield but moved to Portland before the war. I'll bring her letters when I come. She is stationed in Hawaii. She sent a small orchid that she had pressed. I found some violets and I am pressing them to send to her.

I'll see you next week. Until then I am impatiently waiting!

Your cousin, Carolyn

P.S. Oh, by the way, my favorite actor is Gary Cooper and I love Frank Sinatra too.

"You liked older men, didn't you? Gary Cooper was probably old enough to be your grandfather!"

"I liked Frank Sinatra's voice, but how I loved his blue eyes!"

"If you can forget old blue eyes, I'll go on with the letters.")

Mansfield, Oregon
July 20, 1943

Dear Patty,

I had so much fun in Nebraska. Richard is really cute. His freckles remind me of Van Johnson's I think he might be getting a mustache. I mentioned that to Mama and she said we need to have our woman to girl talk when we get home. I'm dreading it because I'll be so embarrassed.

It was good to see Grandma and Aunt Opal. Mama was glad to see Uncle Don too It was so good of him to bring you and Callie from Wabash to Omaha. It must have taken a lot of his precious gas rations. Your parents get along so well that I think that they will get back together someday. Grownups are so complicated.

I liked it the day Aunt Opal and Mama took all four of us to the movie theater and we got to see three movies. I liked "Lassie Come Home" best and Jessie liked the cowboy picture. Mama and Aunt Opal got a lot of shopping done before they picked us up. But the best was when we all went to the Orpheum and saw the movie and then saw Spike Jones and his City Slickers. Didn't you love it when they sang "Der Fuehrer's Face"?

I'm glad we learned the verse that said, "When der Fuehrer says ve iss der master race, we heil,

heil, heil right in der fuehrer's face. Not to love der fuehrer is a great disgrace so we heil, heil, heil, right in der Fuehrer's face." But when I got back here, I got in trouble with Grandma Schmidt when I sang it to her. She doesn't like Hitler but she doesn't like it when we make fun of the Germans. I tried to tell her the song was making fun of Hitler not Germans, but she still didn't like it.

I wish we had a place like Fontenelle Park where we could rent tandem bikes like we did there. When the war is over I want to come back to Omaha and go to Fontenelle Park again and ride the tandem bikes and then see the colored waters that you said they had before the war. I'm glad we went there for the 4th of July but I'm sorry they couldn't have the fireworks that they used to have. The picnic was so good. I loved Grandma's fried chicken and Aunt Opal's potato salad. Nothing is better than homemade ice cream. I'm glad I'm not too old to lick the paddles when it's done. It's a good thing there were four of them so Callie, Jessie, and you and I could each have one to lick.

("Does anybody ever get too old to lick an ice cream paddle? Not me!" interrupted Patty.)

When it got dark, it was fun to dance to the band even if we did just dance with each other. Wasn't it fun to ride in Grandpa's rumble seat on the way home? Mama said Grandpa drove like a madman and she said she wouldn't let us ride in that rumble seat again.

I was so sad when we had to say goodbye at the bus depot. We had a hard time finding a seat because the bus was so full of service men. They were all friendly though and even bought pop and candy for all of us, even Mama. They sang songs too. I liked "There's a Star Spangled Banner Waving Somewhere" and "Don't Sit Under the Apple Tree With Anyone Else But Me". It made the time go faster because we sang right along with them. One soldier played the harmonica and he played good enough that he could have been on the radio. At the end, we all sang "God Bless America".

When we got back to Oregon, the ride through the Columbia Gorge was so beautiful. We could see Mount Hood and Multnomah Falls.

Daddy met us in Portland and took us out to dinner. We got home in time for Gabriel Heater's news. Jessie and I were too tired to unpack so we went right to bed.

I thank you again for such a nice time. I'm going to finish this and then ride my bike to the post office and get it in the mail right away.

With love, Carolyn

Wabash, Nebraska
August 16, 1943

Dear Carolyn,

I had a great time when you were here too. I wish it could have been longer. In fact I wish you'd move back here!

When we got back from being with you in Omaha, it was really boring. Janie had gone to her grandparent's house in Colorado and Richard and George and the others must have been gone too because I didn't see anyone for a week or two. All I could do was practice the piano. Oh, I did learn to crochet. I think it is easier than knitting, but I like to do both of them. All I made was a granny afghan for one of Callie's dolls. Since I'll soon be in seventh grade I've decided that I definitely have to give up playing with dolls.

Last Friday Callie and I went to the show. Her friend, Dolores went with us. The show had just started when somebody pulled my hair. I looked back and there were Richard, George, and Fred so they are all back from wherever they had been. I told Richard to cut it out, but he kept pestering me through most of the picture. It was a good show too. It was "My Friend Flicka". Roddy McDowell was in it and he was just as cute as he was in "Lassie Come Home." I really like horse stories. I wish I lived on a farm so we could have one. Anyway when the show was over, the boys followed us home which I didn't mind even if they were a little loud.

The next week Daddy took Callie and me to Bloomfield to spend a week at our Aunt Abby's. Mama and Aunt Ruby were there too. There isn't much to do there, but I still like to go. Did you know that Aunt Abby's house is over a hundred years old? Remember how many times we played hide and seek there. I like that old house except I don't like to be alone in it, because there are noises in it all the time—sometimes in the attic and sometimes in the dark old damp basement.

One day, all of us picked flowers from Aunt Abby's yard. We put them in fruit jars and then we got in Aunt Abby's old Ford and went to the cemetery. They always go while we're here so they can take care of Grandpa's grave. They call him "Papa" instead of daddy like we call our father. I was only one when he died so I don't remember him and Callie wasn't even born yet. While Aunt Abby, Aunt Ruby, and Mama pulled weeds on Grandpa's grave, Callie and I walked around the cemetery reading the gravestones. A cemetery is a good way to practice your arithmetic—especially subtraction! One man lived to be one hundred and one. Some of the graves had a lamb carved on the top of the tombstone. They are for little children. Callie and I would read them and then feel sad for the little boy or girl who was only two or three or four. Just think, they never got to have many Christmas days, or fourth of Julys or birthdays. I guess maybe they get some fun days up in heaven. We saw some graves that had American flags on them. Those are the graves of the men killed in the war. Most of the men from here are in the army. After the flowers were put on Grandpa's grave we went home. We stopped at the Rexall Drug store and Aunt Ruby bought all of us an ice cream cone. Remember how the druggist always puts a cherry on top of the ice cream? I like cherry nut ice cream and Callie always wants chocolate. I think you always liked just plain vanilla, didn't you?

I better stop this letter or you'll get tired reading it. I'm going to go look through my clothes and see if I have anything that is fit to wear to the seventh grade. I'm starting to change and my dresses just don't fit right and you know where!

Love, Patty

"Modern cemeteries aren't nearly as interesting. Most places have flat stones so the caretaker can mow over them. I guess most of the cemeteries are perpetual care now.")

Mansfield, Oregon
September 20, 1943

Dear Patty,

Can you believe we are in seventh grade? I think seventh grade is great. I almost feel like I'm grown up. We have P.E. now instead of recess. We have to dress down and wear white blouses and navy blue shorts. We also have to wear high-top tennis shoes. Ugly, ugly! Mrs. Banks teaches P.E. for the seventh through twelfth grade girls. We get P.E. on Tuesdays and Thursdays when the boys are in shop class. The boys get P.E. on Mondays, Wednesdays, and Fridays. Big gyp! I love P.E. Why should boys get three days and we only get two, but it doesn't do any good to complain. Besides that, I'd like to take shop and instead they say that girls need three days of home economics.

My arithmetic scores were high so I am taking algebra from Mr. Bumper instead of from our homeroom teacher. Mr. Bumper teaches upstairs in the high school. Margaret is in regular arithmetic and she makes fun of Mr. Bumpers "number bums." She is smart enough to be in that class but she doesn't study at all.

No wonder I'm feeling grown-up because Daddy measured me and I am a half inch taller than Mama. Mama says that I am now a young lady and she bought me three brassieres. Grandma Schmidt is making camisoles for me to wear so nobody will notice that I am developing just like you. Mama says blouses are more ladylike than pullover sweaters so I have to only buy cardigans. Oh, yes, we finally had that talk and Mama gave me a box of Kotex and a book about it. It was embarrassing for both of us.

I'm glad the talk is over but I dread the time when I'll have to use them. Has Aunt Opal given you the "talk"? I can't imagine Uncle Don or Nana doing it! And why do they call it a period anyway? It's not the end of a sentence!

Lt. Betty Bell sent me a lei from Hawaii. It was pretty bruised but it still smelled wonderful. It made Billy Andrews sneeze so the teacher made me put it on her desk. It is hanging in my closet now so all my clothes will smell like Hawaii. Lt. Bell said the hospitals in Hawaii are full of wounded soldiers and sailors. The war is awful. I hate to watch the newsreels in the theaters. Last week I saw "Heaven Can Wait". It was so funny. "This is the Army" is coming next week.

I hope you like seventh grade as much as I do. Tell Richard hello for me. I still think he's growing a mustache.

Love, Carolyn

"No way did Richard have a mustache then. He never liked a mustache even when he grew up!")

Wabash, Nebraska
October 12, 1943

Dear Carolyn,

I was glad to get your letter and read about how it is in your seventh grade. Ours is kind of the same except we have just one teacher except for music and P.E. Our P.E. uniforms are just like yours except we have black shorts and white blouses. So far we have been playing volleyball. I'm short so I usually have to be in the back or middle row. Speaking of short—you said you were taller than your mom but you didn't say how tall that was. I'm only five feet two but that is taller than Mom because she is only five feet tall. Since she's a twin of your mom I suppose your mom is about that size too. Anyway I like volleyball. We have P.E. twice a week and music twice a week. I'm singing in the girls' glee club and also in a sextet that is three girls and three boys. I get to sing alto and that's fun.

Callie is all excited because their class each wrote to a serviceman and yesterday she got an answer. He said he couldn't tell her where he was but he really liked getting mail and he hoped she would send him another letter. He said he was from Ohio and lived on a farm there. Our class didn't do that when we were in fifth grade.

Yes, Mama had "the talk" with both Callie and me. I guess it is all part of growing up. Callie and I said, "Oh, that's what they are!" when she told us about the Kotex. We laughed and told Mama that when I was eight and Callie was six, we went with our friend to a restroom and saw a machine for Kotex. Our friend, Shirley, had a nickel and the machine said five cents so we put the nickel in the machine. When a Kotex came out we didn't know what it was. We took it with us and on the way home we had to cross over that bridge over Sherman Creek. We stopped and decided to make boats out of the Kotex so we tore it up into 6 pieces and dropped them in the creek and watched them float away. Now we know better. And the girls here don't call it "period". They say, "Grandma's visiting." Of course if Grandma was really visiting, I don't know what they would say!

Yesterday we had an assembly at school. Our junior high band played (they are really terrible but they are getting better!) and then we all sang "The Star Spangled Banner" and said the salute to the flag. The principal read the names of all the men from Wabash that are in the service. He said we could all help them win the war by bringing scrap metal to the school. Then it would be sent away and melted into steel to make tanks and guns and ammunition. Then we all sang "God Bless America" before we went back to our rooms. I don't think we're having a contest. We just want to see how much scrap metal we can bring. It will probably be snowing here soon so Janie, Richard, Fred, and I decided we'd go hunt for scrap this weekend. I wonder if we can make as big a pile of junk scrap as you did in Oregon when you made that metal Scrappo! I don't know how much we can find because everybody's been trying to save it.

I think Richard is cute too but I don't think he's growing a mustache yet! Since he is blond it will be hard to tell. He is getting taller and bigger. He's grown a couple of inches since last year so he's four inches taller than I am. Janie said that he's getting too tall for me and she thinks she should be his girl. I think she is kidding!

I've got a great idea to make money for war savings stamps. I'll tell you about it in the next letter, after I've talked it over with Janie and some of the other girls.

You didn't mention Jackson even once in your letter. Isn't he still the one you like?

Write soon.

Love, Patty

Mansfield, Oregon
November 5, 1943

Dear Patty,

Halloween was so stormy that Mama wouldn't let us go out. Trees were blown over and a branch from the big oak fell on our woodshed. We stayed home and made popcorn balls. Mama had made doughnuts so we had apple cider and doughnuts too. It was a very quiet party. I hope you had a more rowdy time!

We had class elections and I'm the class secretary. In answer to your question about Jackson, I'm not sure if I still like him or not. I hardly ever see him or talk to him except in Math Club. He is Mr. Bumber's pet so he won't even look at me or talk to me, much less pass me a note.

Have you ever been a teacher's pet? I haven't and I don't know why. I always get my homework done and I never cause any trouble. I'm not sure what you have to do to be a teacher's pet. Maybe I'm lucky that I'm not since I don't have to act like Miss Perfect all the time.

Our class is putting on a play about the first Plymouth colony. I'm going to try out for the role of Goodie Bradford, the governor's wife. There is a lot of memorizing because she has a big speaking part. I've been practicing my old English. Jessie is annoyed with me because I've been calling her thee and thou.

The American Legion is taking a box of Christmas cookies to the veteran's hospital in Portland in December so Mama, Jessie, and I are going to make pinwheel cookies to help fill the boxes. It is so sad to think of how many service people are in the hospital. My pen pal, Lt. Bell, is being shipped back to Oregon to work in the Portland veteran's hospital. Maybe she won't need a pen pal anymore since she'll be close to her family. I'm glad she is back here but I'll miss the letters from Hawaii.

That's all my news for now. Love, Carolyn

Wabash, Nebraska
December 15, 1943

Dear Carolyn,

We stayed up late listening to the radio to find out about the election. Nana is such a Republican that she was really upset when Roosevelt was elected again. In fact she doesn't even like it that Franklin Roosevelt's birthday is on the same day as hers—January 30th. I don't remember any other president so it seems to me that he will just be president forever.

Remember in my last letter I told you I had an idea about how to earn some money? Well, it was to have several of the girls in our class put on a program and charge something for it. When I talked to Janie and the other girls in my class, they wanted to do it but were full of questions like where should we have it and what will we do? Sally said that I should go talk to Miss Darby because she might help us. She works for the draft board so Callie, Janie and I went up to see her. We asked her if she knew where we could have a show and also if she would play the piano for us. Remember she's the one who plays the piano at Sunday School sometimes. She said she would see if she could get the VFW hall for us and that she would play the piano. After we got home we planned the program. We were going to have a play about the Revolution. We looked in Childlife and found a play about George and Martha Washington that would be okay. In the play we dance the Virginia Reel. We had just learned it in school. Sally B. who is a little boy crazy wanted to ask the boys to help us, but the rest of us said no. We didn't want the boys in the program because we figured they would just fool around and not be a big help. We had to have four men to dance the Virginia Reel with four ladies so four of us had to agree to be men for the dance. I said I would and I talked Janie and Sarah and Esther into it. Callie wanted to but since she is smaller than we are I didn't think that was good. To make the story short, we practiced almost every day for 2 weeks. Richard, Fred, and the other boys kept trying to look in the windows to see what we were doing. Finally we told them that if they'd sell tickets for us, we'd let them watch. Miss Darby had some tickets she said the Elks donated to us and the boys took them and sold most of them. We charged twenty-five cents for the grown-ups and ten cents for kids. The night we had the show, the hall was packed, mostly with our mothers and fathers, grandparents, and of course the boys and their friends. We had pretty good costumes and we'd put flour in our hair to look like the wigs they used to wear. The play and the dance went okay although quite a bit of the flour was falling off our hair. We ended up by singing all the songs of the services (except the coast guard because I still didn't know that one.) Callie and I twirled our batons and Miss Darby played and the other girls sang. Callie and I each dropped our batons once or twice but everybody clapped anyway. The last thing was all of us and the audience sang, "God Bless America" and we all went home. The next day we divided the money. Each of us got $3.75 and we all promised we would use it to buy war savings stamps at school.

Speaking of programs, I hope you got the part in the Thanksgiving play that you wanted.

Yesterday, Janie said to me, "It's a good thing you asked Miss Darby. She probably wouldn't have done it for anybody else."

I said, "What do you mean?" but Janie wouldn't tell me.

What do you think she meant by that?

Callie and I are getting excited about Christmas. We're going to have it here with Daddy and Nana and then ride the train to Omaha to spend some time with Mama. We're getting our tree in a couple of days. I just love the smell of those balsa trees! I'm glad we don't have to wait for the tree until Christmas morning like we did when we were little and we never saw the the tree until we got up on Christmas day. Daddy and Nana are probably glad too because this way we help decorate it.

Have a merry Christmas!

Love, Patty

("How naive we were then! I had no idea that Daddy and Miss Darby were going together."

"Yes," said Carolyn. "I kept thinking your mom and dad would get back together because they got along so well."

"Oh, they were divorced by then, but I guess I was in denial. Hope springs eternal, you know!")

Mansfield, Oregon
January 20, 1944

Dear Patty,

I didn't get the part of Goody Bradford. I played an Indian squaw so I got to come to the feast barefoot. I wore an Indian dress and a feather headband. Grandma embroidered and beaded the dress so it was pretty. I wanted to wear moccasins but the store didn't have any. "It' s the war!" the shoe man said.

Your play sounds like it was a lot of fun. Did you make scenery for it?

We really had a full house for Christmas this year. It was cold enough to snow but the sky was clear. I miss snow at Christmastime more than ever. We had everyone over for both Christmas eve and Christmas day at our house this year. Everyone stayed overnight. It really was a lot of fun. Christmas eve we all went to Christmas Mass except for Daddy, Uncle Klaus, and Mr. Macintosh. When we came home, Santa had come and we got to open presents. Jackson and Johnny got sleeping bags for Christmas because they are boy scouts and are working toward a camping badge. I think I would like to have a sleeping bag, but I loved what I got. It was a fountain pen and a set of drawing quills, ink, and bristol board from Grandma and Grandpa Schmidt. Grandma is teaching me how to use them. I didn't know she was an artist until this Christmas.

After all the presents, Jessie, Jackson, Johnny, Uncle Klaus and I made up beds on the floor by the Christmas tree. It was so nice to go to sleep and smell the wonderful pine smell from the tree.

My baby cousin Jimmy is eight months old now. He is so cute. Aunt Maude and Uncle Klaus are so proud of everything he does. When they come to our house, Jessie treats him like he is one of her dolls. One day Jessie and I got to watch him while Mama and Aunt Maude did some shopping. We found out that not everything he does is cute. I had to change his diaper. Jessie had to hold him down because I was afraid I would stick him with a pin. I couldn't get the diaper tight enough so it kept falling down. We got some wide elastic and made elastic suspenders for his diaper. It looked strange but it worked. The first thing Aunt Maude did when she got home was to re-diaper him. If I ever get married, I'm going to adopt older children that aren't in diapers!

Daddy's boots were stolen, can you believe that? He brought them to Mr. Baltzer, the shoe cobbler to be resoled. The next day Mr. Baltzer called Daddy to tell him that someone had broken into his shop and stolen all of the boots. Daddy doesn't blame Mr. Baltzer because the shortage of leather have made it so hard to get shoes. Mama feels smart because she bought extra shoes and boots before rationing began. So Daddy does have another pair of boots but the ones that were stolen were his favorites.

That's about all the Oregon news I have for now. I'm anxious to get your next letter so you can tell me what Janie meant.

Love, Carolyn

(Carolyn shook her head. "Imagine stealing boots from a shoe repair shop. Most stories of that time were of heroes, but there were some, even then, who resorted to crime.")

Wabash, Nebraska
February 18, 1944

Dear Carolyn,

I'm sorry to say that now I know what Janie meant. I guess everybody knew except for Callie and me. To start at the beginning, I guess I didn't tell you that Mama and Daddy's divorce was final last November. I didn't tell anyone because I kept hoping that they would change their minds. I'm still hoping for that even though I found out that Daddy is dating Miss Darby. That's what Janie meant! She thought Miss Darby would do things for me because of Daddy. I think Janie told me a few months ago that they were dating but I didn't believe her and forgot all about it. Last Friday night at the movies, I found out that it was true. We were sitting in the back and the boys were behind us, whispering to us, etc. You know how they are! All of a sudden I looked up and there were Daddy and Miss Darby being led down to the middle of the theater by the usher. I know he must like her because he hates to go to the movies and there he was! Janie looked at me and poked me in the ribs. I nodded but I couldn't say anything because I was too upset. Anyway, I still haven't given up. Callie and I both say we are still hoping that we'll all be together again someday.

A good thing that happened was that Callie had a great birthday party on Valentine's day. That's such a great day for a birthday. Nana had a party for Callie and she got to invite all the girls in her room. Nana made an angel food cake from eggs she had been saving. It was really good. Daddy made some good ice cream too. Callie got a pretty new dress, a dollar, and socks from Mama and she sent me socks and a dollar too. I always get to have a party too, but having one on Valentine's Day is more special!

Now that we're seventh graders we didn't have a Valentine's Day party, but when I looked in my desk on Valentine's Day there was a pretty valentine with a cupid and a big heart from guess who. I think I know who guess who is, but I could be wrong.

You are lucky to have a baby like Jimmy in your family. We don't have any babies in the family right now. Our two cousins are five years old, so we can't carry them around like we used to. We don't get to see them much anyway since they live in Omaha. Callie and I used to argue about who got to push them in their buggies. There aren't even any babies on our street. Speaking of babies, Esther hadn't ever written in my autograph book so I gave it to her to write in. She wrote, "First comes love, then comes marriage, then comes Richard and Patty pushing a baby carriage." I hadn't heard that one before. So I wrote in her book, "Esther and Donald sitting in a tree, K-I-S-S-I-N-G."

Another gold star is hanging in a window in our town. The son of our friends, the Bishop's, was killed somewhere in the Pacific. I feel so sorry for them. When do you think this war will be over? I hope it is soon. I am so glad that Daddy couldn't go because of his blind eye. I'd be worried about him all of the time. I know Janie is worried about her brother. He was home on a leave in January. He may get to stay here in the United States and be an instructor for new soldiers. Janie hopes so and so do I.

I'm sorry about your Daddy's boots. I hope they find the person that stole them and your dad gets them back again.

Write soon.

Love, Patty

("*Times were so different. I remember silent prayers at school for the men and women in the service No way could that happen now!*"

Carolyn nodded. "Do you remember the Sears Christmas catalogs where they had WAVE and WAC uniforms for kids? I wanted one so badly but my folks didn't think girls should be soldiers or sailors.")

Mansfield, Oregon
March 21, 1944

Dear Patty,

Wow! I can't believe your dad is dating Miss Darby. I think Janie is wrong. I think Miss Darby would have helped you even if she wasn't keeping company with your father.

We have had terrible winds and the most fearsome looking skies. Mama says that in Nebraska when the skies look like that everybody heads for the storm cellars.

The daffodils bloomed but then the winds and rain hit and now they look like someone trampled them to the ground.

I finally filled my savings stamp book and turned it in for a savings bond. I spent $18.75 and in ten years it will be worth $25.

Remember Mr. Hamlin who joined the army? Well, he was wounded and lost his left leg and is now recovering at the veteran's hospital in Portland. He will be teaching 8th grade next year so he will be my teacher. He has received so many medals for bravery. Everyone in my class is so excited that he will be back. I hope he is as good a teacher as Mrs. Snyder is this year. I told her about the play you put on and she thought it would be a good project for our class. We had to decide the ten most important events in American history. We divided up into ten groups who each wrote a five-minute skit on one of the events. We started with the Jamestown Colony and the last one was about the future after the war will end. Margaret, Bobby Banks, and I wrote that one. Oh, I almost forgot. We had to find an appropriate song for each skit or we could write one. We wrote one to the tune of "Over There." It went like this: "Home again, home again, we are safe, we are sound, we are free. We won this battle, we won it fairly, and our troops are home and the world is saved forever now again."

Since we were the only ones to write our own song, the rest of the class sang and I played the piano. Mama and Daddy said it was the best play they had ever seen.

I heard Daddy talking to Uncle Klaus about the war. They are worried about our German family who are still in Germany. Germany is getting bombed every night, just like the Naxi's bombed London at the beginning of the war. At the movies the "Time Marches On" shorts show the bombing. It must be awful for the people on the ground.

Valentine's Day was great this year. We had a roller skating party for 7th through twelfth grades in the old gym because the floor is going to be refinished. I skated with Jackson to the slow music but the fast skating music scares me. It was a lot of fun. We had cookies and ice cream floats that the high school home ec classes served.

Did Callie get the hat that Jessie knitted for her? Can you tell that purple is Jessie's favorite color?

Enough for now.

Love, Carolyn

("Can you still sing that song, Carolyn?"

"I guess I could, but I won't! Wasn't it wonderful how patriotic we were and how we all worked together! We thought that all Germans and Japanese were evil, but now Japan and Germany are friends and allies.")

Wabash, Nebraska
April 27, 1944

Dear Carolyn,

Well, Easter is over. Because of the war shortages Callie and I didn't have any new clothes. It was okay though because nobody else did either. Mama did send us each a cute new dress that she had made out of material from two dresses that Aunt Ruby didn't wear anymore. They were more for school though so we wore our old Sunday dresses. The day before Easter Callie and I boiled and dyed eggs. We got Daddy and Nana to each dye one. Nana's was a pretty red one, but Daddy dipped the egg in every color and so it came out halfway between gray and black. He said he likes black. That night I hid half of the eggs for Callie in the dining room and Callie hid my half of the eggs in the living room. I know we're too old for the Easter bunny stuff, but it's fun to do so we do it. After finding the eggs and breakfast we went to Sunday school and also stayed for church with Nana because it was Easter.

I just have a couple of pages left in my War Savings stamp book and then I can turn it in for a $25 bond too. Of course it won't be worth $25 for ten years and that seems like a long time. I'll be twenty-two years old. Do you think the war will be over by then? I hope so, for goodness sake!

I watch "The March of Time" before the movies too. It seems like things might be going a little bit better for us. Are you still having blackouts and air raid drills?

It is hard for me to be around Miss Darby now, because I know that she dates Daddy. It just doesn't seem right. Of course she is always nice to Callie and me, but she is nice to the other girls too.

Mama says that she is moving to Florida to work at a shipyard that is building ships for the navy. She says she wants Callie and me to come spend the summer with her when school is out. That is exciting but kind of scary too because it will just be the two of us going clear across the country to Florida on a bus. Daddy is thinking about it. He thinks it would be good for us to see another part of our country but he's not sure he wants us to go that far away.

We seventh grade girls have decided that we are too old to take May baskets around but I'm helping Callie make hers. This year we're making cute umbrellas out of crepe paper and the handles are pipe stems. We're going to pop popcorn to put in them and maybe Daddy will let us buy some jelly beans to put in them too. I probably will help Callie take them to the houses of her friends.

It is less than a month until school is out. Then we may be on our way to Florida. I wish you could come too!

Love, Patty

("May baskets were an important part of spring back then. Now you never hear about May baskets anymore," Patty added.)

Mansfield, Oregon
May 19, 1944

Dear Patty,

Florida sounds so great. I envy you. I bet you'll meet a lot of famous people there. I wish I could go to Florida.

School is almost over here. Our spring festival was fantastic. We had an oceanic theme. Our class sang and danced to a song called Codfish Ball. We wore mermaid and merman costumes and sang "Come along and follow me to the bottom of the sea. We"ll join in a jamboree at the Codfish Ball."

My dress was yellow and covered in yellow scales. Our tails dragged behind us on the floor. My dance partner was Melvin Anderson. He's so mean. He kept stepping on my tail at the dress rehearsal until

Mr. Humphrey took him by the ear into the hallway. After that he was a real gentleman.

I think I might like to be an actress. I wish I could sing like you and then I could be another Katherine Grayson.

You know what we should do when our savings bonds mature? We should cash them in and travel all around the world. If the war is over by then, that is!

("I wonder how far we'd get on that $25 from our war bond. Not far even back then," Patty observed.)

We had a flu epidemic and three eighth grade girls couldn't do the Maypole dance so three seventh grade girls got to fill in for them. I was taller than most so I was chosen as one of the three. We wore formal dresses. The eighth grade boys escorted us to the Maypole and then we wove the ribbons around the pole to music. After we had unwound the ribbons the boys met us and escorted us back to our seats. (And NO, Jackson was not my escort. My escort's name was Rodney) Mrs. Snyder was in charge so none of us dared to make a mistake.

Mama graduates in June. I hope you'll get to come out for that.

Write soon.

Love, Carolyn

(You know we never did the Maypole back in my town in Nebraska. Does anybody do it anywhere now?" observed Patty.)

Jacksonville, Florida
June 29, 1944

Dear Carolyn,

I'm sorry this letter is so slow in getting to you. There has been so much going on that I just didn't have time to write.

Mama wanted to come out for your mama's graduation but she couldn't since she was starting a new job in Florida,

You can see by my address that Callie and I are now in Florida with Mama. We are living in an apartment at Jacksonville Beach. It is only about four blocks from the ocean and Callie and I and a new friend, Sally, go there every day. I'll tell you more about that but I want to tell you about the bus trip.

Daddy took us to Omaha and put us on the bus for Jacksonville. The bus driver was a nice man and said he would look out for us. There was a change of buses in Chicago but our Aunt Stella met us at the bus station. We went back to her apartment in Evanston. We got to stay with her for three days.

One day she took us on the El which is a train that runs on tracks that are elevated above the streets. Before we went we had to get all dressed up in our best dresses and white sandals. Aunt Stella was dressed up too and had her hat and gloves on. We went to a play called, "The Red Mill." Aunt Stella said that it is called a musical instead of a play. Callie and I both thought it was so good.

Then another day she took us on the El to see the White Sox baseball team play. I liked it but it was a little too long because it was a double header. Aunt Stella is a real fan and writes down what happens in each inning. She never married and so has no children but we like to visit her because she likes to read to us and take us on walks. I liked riding on the El but sometimes we went by places that looked so bad. The people were sitting out on fire escapes and sometimes there were clothes hanging on the lines. Some of the windows were broken and had paper taped over the hole. Aunt Stella said these were tenements and the people there are very poor. I didn't like to go by those places and tried not to look.

When it was time to go on to Florida, Aunt Stella took us to the bus station and talked to the bus driver about watching out for us. Everything was fine until we got to Indianapolis. I guess the bus driver forgot about watching out for us because we had to change buses and he didn't wait to help us at all. It seemed to us there were about a million buses out there. We kind of wandered around and finally found the right one. I was so happy to get on that bus. I didn't tell Callie how worried I was because I didn't want her to cry. The part I liked best about the rest of the trip was going through Kentucky. It was so pretty with white fences around the fields and red roses growing on the fences. I was really glad to get to Jacksonville though and see Mama waiting for us.

We took a bus out to the apartment. It isn't very big but it is big enough for the three of us. Mama goes to work everyday at a big shipyard. She is in the office and does typing and filing. She has a friend that lives in an apartment in the same place where we are and she is the mother of Sally. Sally is a year older than I am. Everyday we go to the beach and spend all day there while Mama is at work. I have been sunburned two times already but I'm hoping maybe I'll get tan. Callie and Sally are already getting a pretty tan.

We have already had a blackout so now I know about them. We pull the shades all down every night but during the blackout we also turn out all the lights and sit on the floor against the inside wall. We stay there until the all clear siren blows.

It is exciting here. I'll tell you more in my next letter. Write soon. My new address is on the envelope.

Love, Patty

("I don't remember blackouts where we had to turn the lights out, but that may have happened in Seattle or in the large California cities."

"One of the things I remember vividly is how many sailors and marines there were on the streets and at the beach. We were never afraid and Mama felt we were safe. How different it is today," said Patty)

Mansfield, Oregon
July 10, 1944

Dear Patty,

It feels so different to be sending this to Florida instead of Nebraska. You're so lucky to get to the beach every day. I'm so anxious to hear more about you, Florida, and Sally.

You really had a wonderful and scary bus ride. I've never been to a musical or a ball game except for the Mansfield Mongoose Baseball team. We call them the Mongeese.

I think I would have died of fright if I would have had to change buses in a place as big as Indianapolis. How did you ever do it?

We camped at the beach for three days over the fourth of July. We couldn't get Dungeness crab because July doesn't have an "R" in it. You can only eat shellfish in a month that contains an "R". I didn't think shellfish could read!

Some people who were camping near us set off fireworks during the day because they still aren't allowed after dark. It was loud but boring. Some of the people there told Daddy that they had news from their son who is on a battle ship in the Pacific. They said that the American forces are pushing the Japanese back and that the fighting is fierce with many casualties. The newsreels don't show any of that so it is hard to know what is happening. When I looked out over the Pacific, it was hard to imagine that such terrible things were happening in the same water where I jump the waves.

I picked strawberries and have enough money for school clothes. I didn't grow much so most of my clothes will still fit.

Grandma Schmidt has a friend at the Pendleton woolen mills who sends her ends and scraps of yarn. Most of the yarn is army green or navy blue since the mills are making blankets for the services. Grandma mixes this yarn with yarn she already has and her sweaters turn out great.

I am picking cherries with Margaret. We have to ride a bus to the orchard and guess what! Mr. Hamlin is the boss and he will teach eighth grade this fall. Margaret goofs around and gets us in trouble. I keep reminding her that it isn't smart to make your teacher mad before school even starts.

Write back soon and I want to hear everything.

Love, Carolyn

("Margaret never cared what other people thought. Isn't it strange how people who don't care what other people think, are so attractive to people-pleasers like me?"

"What did you like about Margaret? She didn't sound like much fun to me."

"She never seemed to have to live by rules. She fascinated me!")

Jacksonville Beach, Florida
August 15, 1944

Dear Carolyn,

I hope Margaret isn't still causing trouble. You don't want your teacher to get bad ideas about you before school even starts!

I didn't tell you that Sally has a big sister. Her name is Ellen and she's eighteen. She has a figure better than Betty Grable almost. Her waist is tiny and her bra size is about 5 times bigger than mine. Anyway, she usually has a date with a sailor or a marine. (There doesn't seem to be many soldiers around here. But there are some French sailors who have funny hats.) Sally, Callie, and I try to follow her around and we do unless she sees us and yells at us. Today we saw her and a tall marine go to the pier at the beach. The pier is covered but extends out into the ocean. A band plays there every afternoon and evening. They were playing "String of Pearls" when we wandered in looking for Ellen. There she was out in the middle of the dance floor jitterbugging. We jitterbugged a little outside the dance floor but the manager came over and told us that we better leave and wait to come back until we are a little older. We hung out around the pier for quite awhile waiting for Ellen and the marine to come out but I guess they were having too much fun dancing and we finally got bored. We walked down the boardwalk looking at the little shops. Usually we don't have any money but today we had enough to buy a chocolate frosty. We went in the water and a wave picked me up and rolled me over. Luckily it pushed me into the sand because as you know, I don't know how to swim. There is a life guard at the beach and I'm glad of that. We were thinking of heading home when we saw Ellen and her marine strolling down the boardwalk so we ran up and said "Hi."

Ellen said, "You three better be getting home. Our mom and your mom will be home soon. Tom, this is my sister Sally and her two friends Callie and Patty."

Tom said, "Hi. I have a sister at home about the same age as you," and he pointed to Callie. "How'd you like a ride on my shoulders. My sister always loved that."

Callie jumped up and down she was so excited. Tom picked her up and put her on his shoulders and he said, "Let's head for your house."

After a block or two Sally and I asked if we couldn't have a ride too so he gave each of us a ride on his shoulders for a block. We wanted to stay with him and Ellen but they told us to go in so we did. Mama wasn't home yet so Callie and I decided to fix supper since she is always tired when she gets home. All we know how to make is macaroni and cheese so that's what we made. With some applesauce and bread and butter it looked good and Mama said it was good too, when she got home and ate it.

Last week Ellen went out with a sailor named Don. He didn't give us a ride on his shoulders but he gave us all a Mr. Goodbar, my favorite candy. I'm hoping Ellen will choose him but Callie and Sally are hoping she chooses Tom.

Now the bad news! Last week we got a letter from Daddy saying that he and Miss Darby had gotten married and that he hoped we would be happy for them. Well, we weren't too happy because now I guess we'll have to give up on Mama and Daddy getting back together. We'll have to pretend that we're happy I guess.

I'm hoping we can go back to Nebraska before school starts because the kids in Jacksonville go to a junior high school and there are a thousand kids in it. I know I'll hate it

I wish you were here!

Love, Patty

(Patty sighed, "How right I was! I did hate it! Luckily it didn't last long!"

"I remember how scared I was when we came to Oregon from Nebraska, but I liked it here right away because it was a small school like the ones in Nebraska.")

Mansfield, Oregon
September 20, 1944

Dear Patty,

You sound like you're having a wonderful time in Florida. I wish I could be there to follow Ellen and her boyfriends. Does her mother know about all the boyfriends?

I was really mad at Uncle Don for marrying Miss Darby. I told Mama and she told me that I needed to learn to keep my thoughts to myself. Are you okay with this now? And how is Callie doing?

You asked about Margaret. Well, let's just say that we're still friends, but barely. Margaret was goofing off and wasn't picking enough beans. We had to pick one hundred pounds to keep our jobs. I picked over two hundred pounds and Margaret picked seventy. She tried to say that we had poor rows but because I made the quota, our row boss, Mr. Hamlin, said she should have made her quota too so she was fired. Of course she blames me. I think she is becoming too wild for me anyway.

I guess I need a new friend.

Mr. Hamlin is a lot of fun in class. He has traveled a lot and tells stories about his travels. He never talks about his time in the army. He was a medic and was wounded so he walks with a limp. It's funny we didn't even notice it in the bean fields as much as we do now. Margaret still doesn't like him. Too bad for her since he's our homeroom teacher.

Do you remember me telling you about Patsy a long time ago? She could never come to our houses to play when we were younger, but now she invited me to her house for a slumber party. She can even go to nighttime events. She is spending next Friday night at my house because the school is holding a carnival. Patsy has a crush on Johnny McIntosh. Maybe that's why she's choosing me as a friend because his twin brother, Jackson still bugs me so I guess I'm still his girlfriend. He's upstairs in the high school so I don't see him during school time.

Our cousin David, called the other day. He is stationed in Fort Lewis which isn't very far from here. He will finish basic training in November. He will get a furlough and since we're so close he is coming here by bus and Aunt Ruby and Uncle Bill are coming too from Omaha. Wouldn't it be great if you and and Callie and Aunt Opal could be here also?

I hope the war will end before David is sent overseas.

I'll close for now.

Love, Carolyn

("Thanksgiving that year was so great. I hope I wrote to you about it in another letter.")

Jacksonville, Florida
October 18, 1944

Dear Carolyn,

I wish I could be there when David and his folks are there. I haven't seen David for ages. He surprised all of us by going into the army as soon as he graduated from high school and I didn't get to see him before he was sent to Washington. Tell him to write and send me his address and I'll write to him. Tell him about Ellen and he'll probably want her to write to him!

She is still keeping us (and Tom and Sam) guessing about who she likes best. I think Tom is the best dancer. We love to go to the pier and watch them dance, but Don is really nice too. And he gives us Mr. Goodbars!

The other night we had an air raid drill with the blackout and everything. It is so scary for Callie and me. Mama says not to worry, but we do. We are right on the coast here so we would be the first place the German planes would cross over. Here we have blackouts from German planes and you are having them to practice in case Japanese planes come. I hope the war ends SOON!

Now the big news! We have one more reason for giving up hope that Mama and Daddy would get back together—Mama is married again too. She married a soldier whose name is Jim. He is a sergeant and is very nice to Callie and me. We have moved from the beach into an apartment in Jacksonville. He lives there too when he can get a few days leave from the army base where he's stationed.

Sally, Ellen, and their mother moved too. They live just a block from us so Sally walks to the bus stop with us and we get to do things together after school.

The worst thing is that we have started to junior high school. I hate such a big school. The only good thing is that we wait for a bus right by a Spudnut doughnut shop (I never heard of spudnut doughnuts before. I guess they have potatoes in them) and they are just putting out the glazed doughnuts as we're standing there. Sometimes Mama gives us each a nickel so we can buy one. They taste so much better when they are still warm.

We may have some good news soon. Jim says that he thinks he is being sent to another base in the west. Mama says if he goes, she will go there too and since they will not have a place to stay it will be better for us to go back and be with Daddy and Nana—Miss Darby too. Well, I can't call her Miss Darby now I guess. I can't call her Mama so I'll call her by her first name. I think it is Louise. I will miss Mama but I will be so glad to go back to Wabash and my friends there. The only friend I have here is Sally and she is in the grade above me so I don't get to see her much. I hate to eat lunch in the cafeteria with nobody to talk to. So I hope my next letter will let you know that Callie and I are going back to Nebraska.

Sally, Callie, and I went to the movies last night. We saw "This is the Army." When it was finished we waited in front of the theater until Mama and Jim picked us up in a taxi. The street was really crowded even though it was ten at night. Almost all the men were either sailors or marines and every once in awhile we would see some French sailors. Those sailors make me think of the movie I saw. It was "Assignment in Brittany" and a French actor was the star. His name is Jean Pierre Aumont and he is so CUTE. I like him even better than Van Johnson! I asked Mama if I can go to the movie again and she said, "Maybe."

I think you need a new friend too. Margaret sounds like trouble. Maybe Patsy can be a good friend now that her folks are letting her do something besides sit at home.

Are you allowed to date yet? Daddy always told me I had to be fifteen before I could go on a date. If you can, maybe you and Jackson and Patsy and Johnny can double-date.

Hope you have a great Thanksgiving with David and his folks. Let me know all about David. I hope he doesn't have to go overseas.

Love, Patty

("That was a tough time for you. You went from two parents to four in just a few months."

"Yes, and nobody likes to be different at that age, and we were the only ones of all of our friends that

had a stepmother and a stepfather. Now I think it is just the opposite. There are more children with stepparents than those living with both of their biological parents.")

Mansfield, Oregon
November 24, 1944

Dear Patty,

We had a wonderful Thanksgiving. David, Aunt Ruby, and Uncle Bill were so happy to see each other. There were so many of us at dinner that we kids ate in the kitchen and the adults ate later in the dining room. I gave David your address and told him you wanted to write to him. In fact I gave him a book I made with family names and addresses. I put Rita Hayworth's name in with a made-up address. I hope he knows it isn't really her address. I put "Ha Ha!" next to it.

Wow! You now have four parents. Talk about a change in your life! Are you okay with stepparents? I can't imagine how I would feel if I had to divide my time between Mama and Daddy.

The eighth grade class took a school bus to Salem to visit the capital and the state prison. We saw the funniest thing. A small truck from Curley's Dairy was being pulled by a horse. Gas rationing must really hurt. We hardly ever drive our car except once in awhile we get to go to the beach.

The visit to the capital was kind of exciting because we got to meet Governor Snell. I had already been to the capital with you when you were here. The penitentiary was depressing. I'm not going to break any laws and be sent there.

Our class had a mock election for president of the United States. We were in charge of it but the whole school voted. Of course Roosevelt won because this is a union town. Dewey should have shaved off his mustache because some kids thought he looked like Hitler. I liked Roosevelt better so I voted for him. I think Daddy did too because I heard him tell Mama that we shouldn't change leaders in the middle of the war.

You're right about Margaret. She is not much of a friend anymore. She's acting creepy. I think she's proud when she's in trouble at school. I'm not exactly avoiding her but I spend more time with Patsy and Darlene, a new girl. Margaret thinks they are boring so now she tags around with her older sister's friends.

I have a big science test tomorrow so I need to close this up and study for it. There are so many formulas to remember and I still have to memorize the atomic table.

I love eighth grade. I hope it's better now for you. Have you made a friend yet?

Write and tell me all about it.

Love, Carolyn

("I was only there from September to December so I didn't make any friends. It was even worse for Callie because I at least had Sally.")

Jacksonville, Florida
December 15, 1944

Dear Carolyn,

I'm writing this on the train so if my writing looks funny, that's because the train is jiggly. Callie and I are singing "Chattanooga Choo Choo" all the time even though this isn't going to Chattanooga! We're heading for Omaha where we'll stay until after Christmas. Then Daddy will come to Omaha and pick us up and take us back to Wabash. Mama is going to stay a couple of weeks longer with Grandma and Aunt Ruby and then head out to California where Jim is stationed. He left for there right after he got us all packed up and on the train. It will be fun to be with Grandma and the aunts for Christmas but I am so happy to get away from that big Junior

High in Jacksonville and be back in Wabash where I know everybody.

Mama said that she voted for Dewey because she thought four terms was too many for any one person. I probably would have voted for Roosevelt because I just think he is going to be president forever, just like a king.

We brought lunch for our first night on the train but since then we have eaten in the diner. We have to change trains in Chicago and Aunt Stella is coming to meet us. We're going to visit her for two days and then head on to Omaha. This year has really been a strange one. We lived in Wabash, Jacksonville Beach, Jacksonville, and now we'll be in Omaha to end 1944. I wonder what 1945 will be like.

It's a good thing I'm too old for Santa Claus because I would be worried he would never find us since we've moved so much.

I kind of hated leaving Sally but maybe we'll write to each other. We didn't need to worry so much about whether Ellen would marry Don or Tom because she surprised us all and ran off and married a rich kid that she met on the beach. He's only 18 so he is younger than her and not yet in the service. We think she just liked him because his family is rich.

The next time I write it will probably be from Wabash. I can't wait.

Have a merry Christmas!

Love, Patty

("Did you keep in touch with Sally?"
"I think we wrote to each other a couple of times and then we quit. I don't know which of us stopped first.")

Mansfield, Oregon
January 20, 1945

Dear Patty,

Christmas day was strange this year. Mama invited David to come and he brought three friends with him. Daddy picked them up in Portland from the train. They were all in uniform and looked so handsome.

Jessie and I have beds in Mama and Daddy's room and Daddy borrowed cots for the soldiers and they are in Jessie and my room. It is different having people you don't know in your house. Tony is from New York city and has the funniest accent. Marvin is from Atlanta and Jake is from Cadillac, Michigan. They took Jessie and me to the movie, "Meet Me in St. Louis." They bought popcorn, candy, and cokes for us. We never get to have anything like that. Then after the movie they bought us an ice cream cone. When we got home, Jessie walked in the front door and upchucked all over the floor. David kept apologizing to Mama and I don't know why. Jessie was the one who got sick. Mama cleaned it all up.

Daddy called on the telephone to Suki's father and told him that the Japanese can return to their homes again. Her father isn't sure they want to return to Mansfield. He will let us know and if they decide to not come back here, we may sell their farm and send them the money. I hope they decide to move back here because I'd like to see Suki again. I'm a little afraid for Suki to come back now though because people still hate the Japanese.

Oh, I got the neatest gift from Tony. It's a ball point pen. You never have to fill it with ink like our fountain pens.

Do you think you'll get to come to California to visit your mother this summer? If you do maybe you can spend some time with us. Let me know how you like your stepmother. What shall I call her? Shall I call her Aunt Louise? I still think of your dad as Uncle Don.

Does it seem like the whole world is on hold right now? David thinks the war will be over before he is sent overseas. I hope so.

Write soon.

Love, Carolyn

Wabash, Nebraska
February 20, 1945

Dear Carolyn,

It is so nice to be back in Wabash with all of my friends. Of course I miss Mama but I just hated not knowing anybody in school. Everybody seemed to be really glad that we're back.

We had a great Christmas in Omaha with Mama and all the aunts and uncles and Grandma. Can you believe it that Patty and I each got a doll!!!! We're both too old for them, of course, but I have to admit that mine is very cute. It has red hair and blue eyes. At least it will stay nice because I certainly won't play with it. I'll set it up on top of my bookcase. My favorite present was a new winter coat and a white stocking cap. The stocking cap has a long tail on it and I think it looks cute. Callie got one too.

We came here on the bus on the 28th of December. Daddy met us and took us home. It was strange to have Miss Darby there. Well, she said to call her Louise so that's what we'll do. She knew we couldn't call her Mama since we already have one. We call Jim, Jim and not Daddy. So you can call them Louise and Jim too. Both of them are good to us, not at all like the wicked stepparents in fairy tales, but it isn't the same as having just your mom and dad with you. You are lucky that your parents are still together.

Nana was still here and had made a great dinner for us. She plans to go to Lincoln next week. She is going to be a housemother at one of the fraternities at the university. I wish she could stay but maybe four women in one house might be too much for Daddy!

Janie came over the very day after we got home and said there was a skating party at Marilyn's pond. Marilyn lives out in the country and her folks let her have ice skating parties at their pond. Janie said we were invited too. Richard's aunt gave all of us a ride out there. I feel so sorry for her because her husband was killed in the D-day invasion. She is only 23 and now she is a widow.

It was a great party. They had built a bonfire near the pond so we could go warm up by it when we got too cold. I'm not too good at ice skating yet. Richard came and asked if he could skate with me and I was glad of that. He is a pretty good skater and so I didn't spend all my time on the ice on the seat of my pants! After an hour or so of skating, we went to Marilyn's house and her mother had hot chocolate and cookies ready for us. Everybody's nose and cheeks were red and when we went in to the warm house they kind of stung, but we soon warmed up.

I got a valentine in the mail from Richard. At the bottom of the card he wrote, "Will you go to the show with me on Saturday night and be my valentine?"

Maybe I can be his valentine but I can't go to the show with him because Daddy says I have to be fifteen before I date. It's okay though because the boys just come sit by us anyway. I'll be fourteen on my next birthday so I have to wait awhile! Does being fifteen suddenly make you grown-up enough for a date?

I hope Suki and her family move back because I know she was a good friend of yours—better than that crazy Margaret!

(Patty stopped and said, "Whatever happened to that crazy Margaret? Carolyn laughed, "After high school she moved to San Francisco and the rumors were that she had become a call girl. I don't know about that because about a year ago I heard from her sister that Margaret was living in Eugene and was a social director at a big retirement home.

"Those poor senior citizens! I wonder what Margaret plans for them!" Patty picked up the letter and began again.)

As for California, Mama wants us to come out there this summer. If we can't come to Oregon, maybe you can come down and visit us there! I hope we get to see each other.

Write soon.

Love, Patty

Mansfield, Oregon
March 21, 1945

Dear Patty,

Spring is here! Hurrah! Winter is so dreary and I hate it when the sun sets at 4:30.

A new girl came to class this week. Her name is Evangelina Morales and she speaks very little English. Her family is from Mexico. Her dad came from Mexico and is a bracero. Since you have no braceros in Nebraska I'll tell you what it is. The braceros are from Mexico and they come here to work in the crops. Now her dad works at a dairy so they have rented a house near ours. My teacher asked me to help her with English and her other assignments.

The other day her mother sent a package of tamales home with me because I have been helping Evangelina. (I call her Eva now.)The tamales were so good and even Grandma Schmidt liked them. Eva has three younger sisters at home and two older brothers who work with their father.

Suki's family decided that they wouldn't come back to Mansfield so Daddy arranged for the McMinn family to buy their farm. Suki wrote a letter to me inviting me to come and visit her in Canada when the war is over. Mama and Daddy said that maybe we could all go. It's just another reason I want this war to stop. We keep reading that Germany is being defeated so why don't they just give up?

Mama is still watching for Japanese aircraft at the lookout station. She watches Saturday mornings. Jessie and I don't have to go with her anymore because we're finally old enough to stay alone. Anyway Grandma Schmidt is usually there. I'm glad we don't have to go because it's no fun in the winter. The place is cold and has to be heated by an old wood stove so someone has to watch the fire to keep the place warm. Before the observer leaves they have to fill the wood box for the next observer.

Jackson and Johnny have become real Dreamboats! All the girls think they are so cute and one of them, Carline, is flirting with Jackson all the time. Johnny keeps letting me know what's going on. Carline is a cheerleader so she gets to ride on the team bus. I'm not really jealous but she does make me mad!

I'm not allowed to date until I'm fifteen either. Do you think our mother conspired against us?

Actually I'm glad! It's easier to tell a boy you're not allowed to date than to say you don't want to go out with them. But I'll never tell that to Mama.

This letter is getting long and I need to get my beauty rest because I'm going on a bike ride with Eva and we're going to go by and watch the boys at baseball practice.

Love, Carolyn

Wabash, Nebraska
April 14, 1945

Dear Carolyn,

I love it in Nebraska when the ground melts, the violets bloom and everything starts to turn green again. We get our spring later than yours but I think our weather gets hotter sooner.

I don't know if I'll follow a recipe again. Callie and I got to do the Easter eggs all by ourselves this year and we decided to do it when Daddy and Louise were at a school board meeting. I read a recipe that said to bring the eggs to boiling and then turn the stove off and leave them in the water until they cool. So I carefully did that with 24 big white eggs. When they finally cooled off Patty and I dyed them and they looked so pretty in the baskets. I was heading for bed when Callie said that she was hungry and couldn't she have just one of the eggs. I said I guessed nobody would miss one egg. When Callie cracked the egg it was all runny. Callie looked so surprised. I was too!

That recipe was nuts! So Callie and I put all of the eggs back in a pan of water and boiled them again. They all turned out kind of pink. We didn't have anymore dye so our Easter eggs were all pink this year. We hid them for each other anyway!

Saturday Janie and I got our bikes and decided to ride out of town to the rock. We got half way there and heard some yelling. Behind us were Richard, Fred, and Charlie pedaling after us. Luckily we had brought a big lunch with us so when we got to the rock we shared it with them. Richard asked me if I'd go to the show with him that night but I had to tell him my sad tale of not being able to date until I'm fifteen. He said he'd come sit by me anyway. I didn't say so, but I thought that it was a good deal for him because it saved him some money. Charles sat by Janie but she doesn't really like him. She likes Jim who is a sophomore. After the show Richard walked home with me. It was a pretty night and I felt a little like June Allyson when he gave me a kiss before I went in. I was right on time so Daddy couldn't say anything.

Daddy says that he thinks the war in Germany may be over soon. I hope so. It has been almost a year since D-Day. He thinks it will last longer with Japan.

I was so sad when I came home from school on the 12th and heard on the radio that President Roosevelt had died. Now Truman is president. I thought Roosevelt would be president forever.

Only a month and a half left of school and then Callie and I will probably take a bus to go out to see Mama in California.

Don't you think Van Johnson is the cutest movie star. He is RUGGED and a real dream boat! Of course not quite as cute as Jean Pierre Aumont!

Write soon.

Love, Patty

Mansfield, Oregon
May 12, 1945

Dear Patty,

I read your letter and nearly split laughing when I imagined Callie's face when she cracked open the almost raw egg. Anyway pink eggs are appropriate for Easter.

Eva gave me beautiful piñata for Easter. The Mexicans celebrate Easter even more than Christmas. I made an Easter bunny cake for Eva. It was a recipe from the Oregon Farm Journal. It turned out really cute. Eva's family were sure happy to get it because they don't get ration stamps like we do so it's hard for them to get sugar. The dairy farmer they work for gives them food from their farm.

Remember Lt. Betty Bell, my pen pal? Last week she came to Mansfield to recruit women to join the WAVES. She stopped by my class after talking to the senior girls. It was real exciting. She is very pretty. The boys in my class told her they'd like to join the WAVES. Eighth grade boys are so STUPID!

Speaking of stupid. We have a No Speak wall with the words we aren't allowed to use at school. We had to look up the word for stupid and write three sentences with synonyms for stupid in them. I used insipid, obtuse, and oblique. Then we had to write the reason we won't use stupid. I wrote that it doesn't define the condition and I got an A. Obviously I still use that word!

Our family was sad too when FDR died. Daddy is worried about Harry Truman. He doesn't think he's presidential enough. Daddy hopes that Stettinius, the Secretary of State, will help Truman until we can elect a new president. I wish FDR could have lived long enough to see Germany defeated. We were happy when they surrendered but we know the war won't be over until the Japanese surrender too.

The church bells all rang when Germany surrendered but like your dad, we're all still worried about Japan. Mama was told to watch more closely now because they are worried about the Kamikaze planes. They have damaged so many of our American ships.

And yes, Van Johnson is adorable. He looks like he is our age but I guess he is much older. Darn it! Oh, well, we can't date until we're fifteen anyway. I haven't seen "Assignment in Brittany" so I don't know what Jean Pierre Aumont looks like.

Write soon.

Love, Carolyn

("Truman had a lot of decisions to make and I understand that he hadn't even been allowed to sit in on the cabinet meetings so he was really uninformed!" said Patty.

"That's right. No one expected him to be reelected. Remember the newspaper that said "Dewey wins?"

"And now many historians think he is one of our best presidents!")

San Diego, California
June 8, 1945

Dear Carolyn,

Well, now we are in California. I have to admit it is nice weather here. It usually is cloudy but warm until around noon and then the sun comes out and it's just right . . . not really, really HOT like it is in Nebraska. Of course I'd rather be in Nebraska because I miss my friends.

We took the train to Los Angeles instead of the bus and then we had to change trains for another one to get to San Diego. We had to sit on our luggage for that short trip because the train was so full of servicemen. The other train was too but we did find a seat together. When we went through North Platte there was a bunch of women there giving sandwiches and doughnuts to all of the servicemen on board. I had heard about them before. There was even a high school band playing. One of the soldiers offered Callie and me a cookie. It was good. We're getting used to being on a train and even changing trains in Los Angeles wasn't too bad.

Mama and Jim have a small apartment. It is in housing that was put up for servicemen and also people working on defense things. There are other kids around. One boy named Charles asked me to go to a movie but Mama hasn't decided if I can go. Charles says that Donny wants to take Callie and Mama is thinking that maybe it will be all right if all four of us go.

Jim is thinking that he may be sent overseas any day now but of course he can't tell us when or where or anything. As that poster in the post office says, "Loose lips, sink ships!" If he goes overseas Mama says she will go back to Omaha and we can go back to Wabash. We are certainly seeing a lot of the United States because of the war but I still wish it was over. Jim thinks that maybe it won't be long now. I hope he is right.

Do you think you can come down here for a week or so, or should I beg Mama to let Callie and me go up to Oregon? It would be fun for you to get to see California too. This isn't Hollywood but maybe we'll see a movie star anyway.

We don't drink water out of the faucet here. The water all comes in big bottles that are put on a stand. It tastes just the same. I'm not sure why nobody drinks water from the faucets. It must be okay because we cook with it and brush our teeth with it. We also get squirted from the hose with it. Charles and Donny squirted Callie and me yesterday afternoon and we got so wet we had to go in and change our clothes. Mama wasn't too happy about it!

Let me know if you can come down here. Mama said we'd make room for you and even Aunt Pearl and Jessie if they want to come too! We'd be snug as bugs in a rug as Nana would say!

Love, Patty

Mansfield, Oregon
June 20, 1945

Dear Patty,

You are so lucky to get to see two oceans. I wish I could have come to Florida when you were there, but I'm fairly sure that Mama is planning to come to San Diego to help your mom get ready to return to Nebraska. I hope we'll go to the beach while we're there AND I hope my swimsuit from last year still fits me!

While she was at the civil air patrol lookout, Mama was told that a church group on a picnic in Southern Oregon found an unexploded Japanese balloon bomb. We thought that there would be news about it in the newspaper, but the only thing we've heard is "if you come across any metal material, notify the police immediately."

I'm so tired of the war. I'm tired of war stories, gold stars, and everything. Mama keeps reminding me of the children in Europe and China who are so much worse off than we are. On Wednesdays we are supposed to meet at the church and pray for the people of China and Europe. They also asked us not to eat any meat or fish on Wednesdays so most of the time we eat macaroni and cheese on those days. We eat fish on Fridays because the Catholics can't eat meat on Fridays. The fresh fish always comes in then. Isn't fish meat? I guess not. I wonder who makes up these rules.

I sent Lt. Bell's address to cousin David. He wrote to her because he's going to be stationed in Fort Lewis for awhile and that's not far from here. Maybe they'll really like each other and get married and we can be in the wedding. Callie and Jessie could be flower girls and we could be candle lighters or Junior bridesmaids.

Write and tell me what clothes to pack in case we get to come

Love, Carolyn

San Diego, California
June 25, 1945

Dear Carolyn,

I'm so glad you're coming! I can't wait! Wait until you go in the Pacific ocean down here. You'll be so surprised at how warm it is.

I'm trying to think of what we'll do. Balboa Zoo is great and we could go to the Navy base so you can see the big ships and because Mama is married to Jim, we could go in the commissary, and Mama said we'd try to go to Tijuana in Mexico. Just think, we'll be in a foreign country!

Bring your swimming suit and your camera. I can't wait!

Love, Patty

Mansfield, Oregon
July 20, 1945

Dear Patty,

I had so much fun in San Diego. Thank you so much! Mama couldn't believe how beautiful the bougainvillea is. It was everywhere. Mama is trying to root the geraniums that she brought from the mission. Grandma is horrified that Mama took starts from a Catholic mission even though Mama explained to her that the monk there gave them to her. It is almost funny because every time Grandma looks at the plants she clucks her tongue and shakes her head to say "No."

Besides getting to see you, my favorite part of the vacation was the time at the beach. You were right! I couldn't believe how warm it is compared to the Pacific up here. Didn't we have fun jumping the waves? It was scary when the lifeguard ordered us out of the water because sharks had been sighted, but it's exciting to think about it now. The ships were so huge! There is something so exciting about the sailors in their white uniforms and those cute little hats. Jessie still beams when she tells her friends about the sailors whistling at us when we went with your mom to the navy base. I think they were whistling at us because our mothers are too old and our sisters are too young! Besides they yelled, "Hubba, hubba!" and we were the only ones wearing short shorts.

Charles is cute but he's too young for you. I guess the sailors are too old but they sure are cute! Hubba, hubba!"

I keep the picture of us in Tijuana, Mexico on my mirror. I love the marionettes, the big sombreros, and the matching jackets that we bought. The street merchants scared me at first when they grabbed our arms trying to get us to come into their store. Jessie and I keep saying, "Come "een", Senorita. Thees is the place! We have what you need!"

The sombreros were a problem on the train going home because there were so many soldiers and sailors that it was hard to find a place to sit. Finally Jessie and Mama found a seat together and I found a seat by Vernon Watson from Tacoma. He was so funny when he wore my sombrero and spoke funny Mexican. I know Mexican is really a Spanish language, but he was so funny that even the conductors were laughing.

Everyone here loves my jacket and wants to wear it. I hate it when my friends want to trade clothes.

I miss all of you so much. Thank you again for the wonderful time in San Diego.

Love, Carolyn

("How times have changed," said Patty. "It was so unusual then to hear a foreign language, but now in many places you can hear many different languages.")

San Diego, California
July 30, 1945

Dear Carolyn,

I was so glad you and Aunt Pearl and Jessie got to come see us and help us pack.

We expect to leave in a week or so. In the meantime we're living out of our suitcases because we shipped a lot of things back to Nebraska. Anyway it's a good thing this place was furnished so we didn't have to worry about sending the furniture back.

You're right! Charles is too young but he was fun to be around. It doesn't matter anyway because we'll soon be on our way. We're taking the bus this time instead of the train.

Playing in the ocean was fun, except I didn't like it when that wave rolled me over and I got sand in my mouth. Mama and Aunt Pearl liked the beach too and they looked pretty good in their new swimsuits. I'm not sure if those sailors were whistling at you and me or at them. I think we're getting to the age when they might have been whistling at us.

It was more fun at the zoo because all of you were along. You and I could look at what we wanted to look at and Callie and Jessie did what they wanted. I think Mama and Aunt Pearl did more talking than looking. Mama says that twins are really close so they have missed each other a lot. *("They were really close," said Carolyn. "After your mother died, Mama was never really happy again. And she died the next year.")*

I guess the best part of your visit was going to Tijuana. I had never eaten a taco before and it was so good. I'm glad Mama bought us those embroidered felt jackets with the pictures of things in Mexico on it. I kind of wish I'd gotten another color besides red. It's so bright that I'll probably not want to wear it. You wore yours so I guess I can wear mine but my red one is much brighter than your blue one! Maybe I'll wear mine on the bus. I don't know what the kids in Wabash will think of it. I'm glad we all got our pictures taken with the donkey and the cart and wearing those sombreros. I'm putting mine in my album but maybe first I'll put mine on my mirror like you did. That was our first trip to another country Maybe, sometime after the war we can go to Canada together.

Well, the next time I write it will be from Nebraska. By the time we get there it will be only a week or so before school starts. Just think, we'll be high school! If you write to me before then you can send it to our old address and Daddy will save it for me.

Write soon.

Love, Patty

("How many countries have we visited now?" asked Carolyn.

"I've never counted, but isn't it amazing how world travel expanded after the war?"

"Our G.I.s brought back so many stories and then there were the war brides that piqued our interest in foreign travel."

"I guess war does bring a few positive things.")

Mansfield, Oregon
August 25, 1945

Dear Patty,

I prayed every day that the war would end and now that it has I can hardly believe that it's real.

The day the war ended one of the farmer's west of Mansfield drove his flatbed truck into town with a scarecrow on it that was supposed to be Tojo. He brought boxes of spoiled apples, tomatoes, and plums and everyone threw the fruit at the scarecrow. I was with Grandma Schmidt so I didn't get to do any of the throwing. I'm glad I didn't because it soon got really messy. The boys began throwing fruit at each other and anyone else they knew. Grandma made Jessie and me come with her so we didn't get to see much of it. The newspaper said it was a grand but messy celebration. We could hear church bells ringing and horns honking. It gave me shivers!

When we went home Grandma made a big pot of goulash and roasted a turkey so we had a big party that night in our backyard. We kids played softball until dark and then Uncle Klaus played the guitar and we sang patriotic songs like "God Bless America, "You're a Grand Old Flag" and all the military songs. Then we sang some old songs like "You are My Sunshine," and "The Yellow Rose of Texas". It was after midnight before everyone went home. Grandma and Mama put the leftover food in the fridge and put the dishes in the sink until morning. I couldn't believe it! I don't think Mama has ever left the dishes before!

David came down from Fort Lewis yesterday and asked if he can stay with us until he can find a place after he gets out of the service. He wants to go to the same college that Mama graduated from. He and Lt. Bell are still going together. It sounds serious. She wants him to finish college. If they wait to get married until after he graduates, we'll be old enough to be bridesmaids.

Mama is thrilled because she has signed a contract to teach typing and business in the high school next year. I overheard Mama and Daddy talking about taking the train to Nebraska for Christmas this year. Keep your fingers crossed! Wouldn't it be fun to be together for Christmas again?

Write soon.

Love, Carolyn

("And didn't we have a grand time that Christmas? Everybody was so happy that the war was over. We had so much to be thankful for that year. And we even had a white Christmas for you!"

Carolyn nodded, "That was the best of all. Nothing like a white Christmas to put you in the mood. Remember, that was when we learned to play pinochle.")

Wabash, Nebraska
September 10, 1945

Dear Carolyn,

What a bus trip home we had! When we got into Reno we looked out of the bus window and saw people running around in the streets and yelling.

We knew it was something good because everyone was laughing and smiling. We were supposed to have a forty-five minute stop there for dinner so we all filed off the bus asking, "What's going on?"

"The war's over!" the bus driver said. "Japan has surrendered!"

Then we all hugged each other and laughed. Mama was happy because she knew Jim would be coming home soon. We got a booth in the bus restaurant right away because almost everybody was out celebrating. When we got back on the bus everybody couldn't stop talking about it. In fact that's all everybody talked about all the way to Omaha.

We stayed a few days with Grandma and the aunts and then Mama put us on the bus to Wabash. Janie came over right away and we went for a hike to the rock. We talked about Richard and the other kids. She said he had been playing American Legion baseball and working on a farm so she hadn't seen him very much.

It sounds like the end of the war was really celebrated where you are too! I'm glad they weren't throwing rotten fruit in Reno.

I hope David and Lt. Bell do get married. You can hint to him that we'd like to be bridesmaids.

School starts early here because in October the school lets the boys go help harvest the corn. The very first day, Mrs. Lambert, the music teacher, got us all together and handed out a song for us to learn. We practiced quite awhile because the next day we all went to the Methodist Church and everyone was in the churchyard. The minister prayed a thanksgiving prayer of thanks that the war was over and then we all sang the song we'd practiced. It was "Ring Out Sweet Bells of Peace!"

Now that peace is here we can think about what a great time we'll have. We'll finish high school, go to college, get married, have babies, and have a great life! I can't wait!

Write soon!

Love, Patty

("And it has been a great life," said Carolyn.")

Afterward

Patty and Callie finally realized that their mother and father were never going to get back together. When they talked about it, they always said that they were glad that at least both their mother and father married people that were kind to them. "I'm glad I wasn't a Cinderella," Callie often said.

Patty graduated from Wabash, Nebraska high school in 1949. She and Richard were high school sweethearts and became engaged when Richard enlisted in the navy during the Korean War. Patty went to the University of Nebraska majoring in Education. She taught at a small school in Nebraska until Richard came back from Korea. They were married in the summer of 1953. She got a job in Lincoln teaching at one of the grade schools so that Richard could attend college. When Richard graduated he got a job as a high school teacher in Wabash. Teachers were needed to teach the swelling numbers of students—the baby boomers. Patty taught a year and then she quit to raise their their first child—Tom. Sally, Paula, and Mitchell arrived in quick order to also swell the growing number of children in every part of the United States. On their street of eight houses, there were 25 children of school age or younger. When all the children were in school, Patty went back to teaching. Patty and Richard took turns going to the children's conferences, Little League games, and other sporting events. It was not easy to be present for all their children's needs and to spend time on their classes and the needs of their students. During the summer they took turns getting the college credits they needed to keep their work updated. They tried to take a trip each year and often went to Oregon so that the children could learn to know their second cousins, Jessie's three sons, and later Carolyn's twin stepdaughters.

Both of them retired in 1994. For a couple of years they enjoyed going to Elderhostel and especially enjoyed one at Mesa Verde. By then they had 10 grandchildren and enjoyed again going to Little League games, school programs, and piano recitals. In 1999 Richard began to be short of breath. He had an appointment with the doctor on a Thursday but died on his way there while stopped at a stop sign. Patty did not know what to do, alone, after forty-six years of marriage. At first she would not go anywhere but urged by her friends she again began to socialize and meet with them, many whom were also widowed. Beginning in 2000 she drove with friends to many places she had wanted to see. When she met Carolyn to reread their World War II letters, she was feeling quite well and planning how she would spend the rest of her retirement years.

Her sister, Callie moved to Omaha after graduating from college. She worked as a legal secretary. An ambitious young lawyer in her office courted her and they married only a few months after they began dating. Their first years were happy and they had a son and a daughter. The family often went to Wabash where their children and Patty's loved to play together. A trip to Omaha was a treat for Patty's children too.

Callie was dismayed at how quickly her two children grew up and left home to attend college. With them gone, she and her husband realized that they had grown apart and they eventually divorced. Callie lived in their family home for several years before she met the man she later married. It was this wedding that Patty and Carolyn were attending when they met to read their letters.

Carolyn was a freshman at the University of Oregon when she learned that Jackson had been killed in Korea. She was devastated. She took time out from the university and spent the next summer with her grandparents in Germany. While she was there she took pictures of the situation in Germany and how it was divided into east and west sections. When her grandparents and herself were denied a visa to visit relatives in East Germany, she shared with a passion her grandparents sense of injustice. Her letters and the pictures she had taken were published in her hometown newspaper and later published in the Oregonian newspaper in Portland, Oregon. When the wall between east and west Germany came down she rejoiced even though her grandparents were now dead and had not lived to see Germany united again.

That fall, back at the university, she took journalism as well as education classes. She had a hard time deciding whether to become a teacher or a journalist. She finally decided that teaching was where her greatest interests lay. She completed her education requirements with a BA in education and a minor in journalism. After graduating she moved to Portland where she taught English, drama, and literature in several of the high schools. Her interest in writing continued and she wrote several short stories that were published in magazines.

In her late 30s she met a handsome widower with twin teenage daughters. Alexander Godwin was a feature writer for the Oregonian and was writing about the play Carolyn's students were performing. He and Carolyn became good friends and during the next several months Carolyn developed a good relationship with his daughters. By the time Carolyn and Alex married, his girls were happy to have her as their stepmother.

Carolyn's sister Jessie, had married during her college years. She had three sons whom Carolyn adored and spoiled every chance she got. Even though she had no children of her own, her stepdaughters and her three nephews provided her with loving relationships. Often in the summer she and Alex went to Nebraska to spend time with Carolyn and Richard and their children.

Alex died the year before the cousins met in Nebraska to share their letters.

When they met to read the letters Patty and Carolyn discussed and agreed that they had lived in a remarkable time. When they were young much of rural America had no indoor plumbing and many farmhouses had no electricity. They grew up playing outside and making their own games and often their own toys. They had radios but no television. They felt privileged to see the advent of the space age, television, jet planes, microwaves, computers, the internet, and cell phones. The remembered how proud they were when they watched the American astronaut, Neil Armstrong, step on the moon in July of 1969.

They wondered what changes were ahead. Would the twenty-first century bring as many changes to the world as the last century? But whatever lay ahead, Patty and Carolyn agreed that they had lived in a remarkable time.

Authors' Note

The names, characters, and events in this book are fictional, though many of the events actually happened.

Snapshot Memories from WWII

Children loved to dress in military attire. Catalogs such as Sears, Roebuck, carried children sized uniforms for the army, the navy, the WACS and the WAVES.

The toddler above is wearing a hand-made army officer's uniform. The little boy on the right is wearing a sailor's uniform purchased at a military PX.

Scrappo was put together by the Marion County Salvage Committee. This robot actually moved its arms and its mouth. A voice seeming to come from Scrappo, entertained and informed the people passing by.

It was so popular that it appeared in several newsreels.

Above are three of the many patriotic songs that were popular and often played and sung during World War II.

Victory gardens sprang up in many yards and the cooks of the household appreciated cookbooks such as this one, for they offered recipes that were adjusted to the reality of the many scarcities.

United States of America
Office of Price Administration

WAR RATION BOOK No. 3

713222   F

Void if altered

Identification of person to whom issued: PRINT IN FULL

(First name) *(Middle name)* *(Last name)*

Street number or rural route

City or post office _____ State _____

NOT VALID WITHOUT STAMP

AGE	SEX	WEIGHT Lbs.	HEIGHT Ft. In.	OCCUPATION

SIGNATURE _____
(Person to whom book is issued. If such person is unable to sign because of age or incapacity, another may sign in his behalf.)

WARNING

This book is the property of the United States Government. It is unlawful to sell it to any other person, or to use it or permit anyone else to use it, except to obtain rationed goods in accordance with regulations of the Office of Price Administration. Any person who finds a lost War Ration Book must return it to the War Price and Rationing Board which issued it. Persons who violate rationing regulations are subject to $10,000 fine or imprisonment, or both.

OPA Form No. R-130

LOCAL BOARD ACTION

Issued by _____
(Local board number) (Date)

Street address _____

City _____ State _____

_____
(Signature of issuing officer)

Ration books such as this one were issued to everyone, including the children.

CPSIA information can be obtained at www.ICGtesting.com
Printed in the USA
BVOW072235120713

325706BV00001B/2/P